EVERY FIRE YOU TEND

TRANSLATED BY

EVERY FIRE YOU TEND

SEMA KAYGUSUZ

NICHOLAS
GLASTONBURY

TILTED AXIS PRESS

suskunluk

The state of being silent, taciturn, tongue-tied.
There is very little speech in this novel; its two
sections, "Sigh" and "Wail," are sounds we make
when language fails. Mired in the ongoing afterlives
of the Dersim massacres, the characters in this
novel are overcome with *suskunluk*, imposing upon
themselves vows of silence in their grief. In grief,
it feels impossible to speak, to impose the order of
language on the chaos of loss. Silence marks not
the absence of emotion but its acute abundance,
and here, this abundance—this story—combusts in
the loudest silence of writing.

Think of the flame on a candle, which burns it away
from the inside. This motif plays a significant role
in the twelfth-century Alevi-Bektaşi and Sufi poetic
traditions from which this novel draws liberally. As
the wick burns down and the wax evaporates, the
candle burns in on itself, leaving behind a hollow
pillar of wax. The candle's flame may have offered
solace and refuge, may have lit a path, shown the
way; it may have started a great conflagration, may
have burned everything to the ground. And though
the tunneled candle may have tended so many
feelings, sentiments, thoughts, and stories, they are
not harbored in the candle's ever-dwindling remains
but in the flame itself; indeed, they are the flame
itself. *Suskunluk*, too, is a flame.

SIGH

I know your shame.

I carry it with me, that shame, that most private part of you. Ever since I was entrusted with that cryptic emotion, I haven't taken my eyes off of you, off of the historic secret inscribed on your face. Before the mother who bore you and the father who dreamed you up had themselves come into this world, you were already a doleful visage conjured by your ancestors, the final entry in a searing elegy imparted from flesh to flesh. You do not know how to read what is written on your face. You do not know the source of your latent shame, do not know how to speak of it, let alone string its sentences together, and so it weighs on you as an affliction, stunting your growth.

Only in the thrall of emotions you recognize does that writing on your forehead disappear. When your lips curl in contempt, for example, or when your eyes well up with longing, not a single word of shame remains etched on your face. Sometimes, though, when your mind begins to wander and you're torn from this time, unfamiliar emotions envelop you, and you can't remember a thing. That's when I find you, aching from head to toe with the obscure memory of an event you never lived through.

—

This morning when I arrived, you were lost in thought, caught in the cross breeze, on a threshold opening into the depths of your melancholy. Wearied by sleeplessness, your spirit snagged itself upon objects around you: the swaying tulle curtains, the photographs on the wall, the little spider dangling from the web it prudently let loose; it tumbled its way to your body, the home of your introspections, carrying with it all those intimations of the world, while you lay there in bed, passive in body but agonizing in mind, trying to fend off these unwanted intrusions. You spirit had departed to another plane altogether, and you were left suddenly alone, among strangers who wouldn't say a single word to help you. All those strangers standing on the other side of the threshold, wandering the labyrinth of your melancholy, calling you on a journey without return, into the boundless universe of your introspections. One of them, an old woman, her hair so white it seemed ice blue; another, a holy man, his face pallid, sprung from the sanguine legends of the spring festivals. You recognized them both but didn't know from where. The middle door of your introspections opened upon a fig tree. There on that threshold, you breathed in the scent of its bitter leaves, observed its white branches twisting outward, heavy with purple fruit.

You weren't there with me. All I could see in your place was the ache in your bones, the sweat on your hands, and the pain in the hollow of your groin. You were in a wretched state. Your "I" had shrunk in that ancient agony, all the time you'd lived through condensed into a fig seed. Doubled over in bed, you listened to the throbbing of your flesh, afraid to open your eyes, your arms covering your face. You wanted to close the door that opened onto your melancholy. Or perhaps you were desperate to escape, to leap into another time in which you'd never been born and would therefore never die, a realm beyond the world's many insinuations. A centennial distance loomed between us. We stood on the same piece of earth, sundered into different times. I watched you splintering apart. You were the protagonist of an anguished story, borrowing the consciousness of a woman from another time, a victim's consciousness, one that continues to loom large in the present. You mutilated yourself with your self. What's more, you were afraid of a phantom whose fresh sweat you could still smell on your sheets, undeniably tangible and passing through your time. You and your phantom had emerged anew from the Hıdrellez flames.

Let me tell you about the first Hıdrellez flames you ever saw, a story from a time before you existed, when your conscience was just being woven together, some seventy years ago. You were elemental as a new spark, a mad-hot stone in the heart of a fire, a dry branch that crackled with the first lick of flame. Your eyes that watched everything were the silver-dappled stones. You were a place on that mountainside, and you were the otherworldly aura that permeated the place. That day, you were both the burning fire and the person who warmed herself beside it.

Forty people with packs on their backs, weary from walking for days on end, weak from living off only wild spinach, gathered around a fire, taking solace in each other. The children smelled of urine, and everyone, with their shorn clothes and jackets, looked utterly ruined. They hadn't yet realized that they were exiles. The deep guilt of having survived had plunged them into silence. Afraid of stepping back into the nightmarish, bloody landscape that they had left behind, they refused to sleep. Water, fire, and bread had taken on entirely new meanings: water smelled of blood, fire screamed, and bread turned into a sacred pittance they hoped would fall from the heavens.

These people gathered around the fire had lost their fear of dying. Besides, they were so lifeless now that it would be impossible to kill them further. Ever since they'd gotten off the train from Elazığ, their spirits had been utterly numb. As they continued onward, burying those who couldn't withstand the fever and the hunger, the world itself became another affliction. They were like Job, who beseeched God that his spirit had grown weary of his body: all realms known and unknown, all seven tiers of heaven and seven tiers of earth, had become for them no more than a body writhing in pain.

There was a man named Cafer among them. His right eye was wrapped tight with a bloody rag while the other was bright red. As if he had left this eye uncovered not to see but to weep. Swaying back and forth, he began muttering as if speaking to the fire, as if the fire was the only thing that could understand him. Words rolled around in his mouth. "O Hızır," he moaned, "O Hızır, my unseen brother, where are you? At the throne of God, or here on earth? Do you stand before Moses, do you sit beside Gabriel?"

Meanwhile, night was overtaking the land. A deceptive stillness enshrouded everything, the light playing tricks as it reflected off the jagged cliffs. The outlines of the trees on the mountainside slowly became indistinct, and all the pathways and passes disappeared in the twilight. Gathered around the fire, the abject figures melted away, replaced by their black, hunched silhouettes. Cafer's reproachful entreaty to Hızır suddenly coalesced in a rhythmic prayer the forty of them sang together, forging a clandestine bond between serenity and sorrow. They were submitting themselves to their faith in God. There in that leaden stillness, as Cafer's voice filled the air with tension, a girl stood up and calmly brushed off her skirt.

That girl was your father's mother, Bese. Bese had a small beauty mark below her lower lip where her mother would always kiss her, a small gesture of her love. Bese, now the sole survivor of all her extended family. Ever since she had seen her brother's body drifting along the Munzur River, she had taken a vow of silence, to be broken only when absolutely necessary.

Bese began to walk, slowly at first. Nobody gave her a second glance as she wandered into the nearby copse, assuming perhaps that she was going to urinate. If they had only paid heed to the tautness of her back, to her jutting shoulder blades, to the speed with which she was now walking, to the fact that she was no longer limping, they might have realized that hers was a strange departure.

Bese didn't return that night. The others scattered in all directions, setting out to search for the girl. They didn't have the fortitude to lose another, nor could they live with themselves if she had died, if she had fallen somewhere and gotten stuck, and they had left her behind. Wearily, they searched for Bese. When they lost their voices from shouting, they clashed stones together. They shuddered at the calls of birds of prey and started at every rolling stone or rustling branch, and soon, legends about Bese began to circulate among them. One would say that Bese was with them still, only now invisible; another, that she had died long before, but her spirit had only just departed; another still, that she must have gotten mixed up with djinns.

"I don't know anything about djinns," clamored one old woman, "but if we give up on Bese we give up on her entire lineage. I'm not leaving until we find that girl!"

On the morning of the third day, Bese appeared out of nowhere. Half naked, her hair disheveled, her arms and knees bleeding and bruised. Her ribs were pressing into her lungs, so she was barely able to speak. She seemed to have undergone a profound transformation, her timidity abandoned for an air of defiance, a readiness to pick a fight. She shunned

everyone with her intransigence, placing an insurmountable distance between herself and her tribe.
The knowledge that all beings had been leavened by
the same stardust brought her only empty consolation
now. To survive, she needed to approach life differently. Resurrected with a new grief and a new set of
ethics, Bese had been born again, this time through
another wound.

"Where were you?" they asked her.

"I saw Hızır," she replied without hesitation, as if
explaining something entirely ordinary. "He was on
his grey horse, staring at me. He gestured for me to
come, so I went.'"

As she spoke, a profound sorrow spread over her
face, almost identical to the expression latent on
yours. How exactly you're going to step free from this
sorrow, etched as it is into the fabric of your soul, is
something I'm still wondering myself.

Now you've entered the age of figs. You're ready to show and tell all, on the brink of offering your honeyed core to life. You even have a fig tree, there, blocking your living room window. You've learned how to get by on the feeble light filtering through its broad leaves. The tree's shadow casts another dimension into your daily life. At first, anyone who visited you at home would have to listen to you talk at length about it, let you translate for the fig without its permission. In fact, you often got carried away, telling visitors that the fig leaf resembles a giant hand, the hand of the goddess Demeter. You bestowed meanings on the leaves that leaves can't bear. After all, every life is defined by such meanings. And you were defined by figs.

Before you rented your current apartment, when you were wandering from realtor to realtor in Beşiktaş, you insisted that you wanted a small, ground-floor apartment, and moreover, one that came with a fig tree, telling those who looked at you with bewilderment that the time had come to live with a fig tree. As if that sentence made the slightest sense… They gave up looking for a flat altogether, thinking a fig tree was all you were after. Muammer, with his Coke-bottle glasses, was the only realtor who took your request seriously. "I love walnut trees," he told you in his nasal voice, smoothing his hair from its part down the middle. His shoulders were covered in dandruff. You tried not to stare at his yellow teeth as he prattled on about how sleeping under a walnut tree always left him in a gentle daze, waiting patiently for this dull banter to end. The only thing you and Muammer had in common was trees. But your eyes, they couldn't see past figs.

The first thing you did after you signed the lease was name the fig tree in your garden. You called it Zevraki, claiming the name meant both "boat" and "wood." The nickname of an Alevi bard who died long ago. You've always loved the letter Z. Every word that Z passes through seems to you caught in paradox, half dead and half alive. Everything Z touches: azure, zephyr, zero, zenith… Z blazes like fire, freezes like ice. Zevraki, that seemingly musical name, circumscribed the tree, enclosed it in a place oscillating between dream and reality. Ignorant as to the sex of your tree, you attempted to graft it with the name of a poet. It's not natural, what you did. All it does is reinforce the recursive cycle by which civilizations build the logic of their own undoing into their very foundations. Naming something forces it to adapt to you; it is the first step toward domesticating all of earth's creatures, the rageless and meek, the plain and serene. Regardless of the name you gave it, the only thing you will ever see in the tree is a semblance of yourself. I have to admit, though, that the names you come up with do always suit the thing being named. I don't know how you do it, but it seems to me that your naming recreates it anew. Ever since you named the fig tree in your garden Zevraki, I've been drifting upon an ocean, the same poem restless in my mind:

if the waves rose high, higher than the north star, if they

swelled past the limits of the vaulted sky, and if they swept

into even the ninth heaven, surged beyond the throne of

god, still zevraki would remain above the surface of that

vast sea.

How do you think fig trees were born? Did they fashion themselves according to the angle of the sunlight, or to the appetites of the birds and bugs in their surroundings? How did they come into being, and in which time zone? Your Zevraki, for example... When I think about the endless cycle that culminated with Zevraki, I imagine a tendril secreting a milky poison, sprouting from beneath a lapis stone on a silvery Syrian cliffside overlooking the Mediterranean. Long before Adam and Eve covered their private parts with its leaves, it was a bastard that grew of its own accord.

It's almost as if we exist because figs do, think of it that way. The fig is a scion that spread by imagining humans before it had ever encountered them. It conceived of the fire that would fall into the womb of the first woman to eat its fruit, of the moment she splits it with her two hands; it conceived of the thumping that fire would start in her chest, of the sweet ache in her groin; and it conceived of the honey that would flow from her lips upon her first bite, of the carnal prowess of that honey. It wished for men as it grew, men who gathered together to play their frame drums and sing ghazals as they drank rakı distilled from figs; it wished that the songs they breathed into the air would help them reach lovers waiting in the world beyond. It designed roots to spread like vortexes along the surface of the earth, building nests for snakes slithering silently among them. This was how the dual bond between figs and snakes began. Over time, the shadow of the fig tree became the gathering place for punishment and praise, for poison and antidote, for arousal and calm. Eventually, its roots meandered underground. It emerged among humans in strange places, splitting the walls and cracking the foundations of derelict homes across the four corners of Mesopotamia. In time, of course, the fig became something of a demigod. In an age when innumerable gods and goddesses and human-animal hybrids began to converge in the fabric of a singular creator, the fig held its place in the world with a terrifying depravity, a symbol of the singularity in the plural and the plurality in the singular. And so, as the fig became a mysterious creature that consorts with snakes, a creature that sees, that knows, that speaks in whispers to the night, humankind began to treat it like a being from another world.

The Arameans gave the fig its first name, calling it İdra, or spirit, and thus setting it apart. Ever since this naming, *all great adventures have transpired before it.* In fact, the fig tree was the symbol of knowledge in

Hebrew, and from İdra, it grew into a weightier, more sublime concept of wisdom. These letters, portals that open onto all places in the universe, hold the fig's ingenuity. Because of the spell contained in the word İdra, to speak the fig into the world is not only to give voice to the greatness condensed in everything, in water and leaf and stone, from the peach fuzz of human skin to the fur of a leopard; it is also to declare, "There is a beginning." Reverberating in Hebrew, the fig became a sonorous sentence that nobody could grasp in its entirety.

As luck would have it, though, the fig began to fall from favor once it gained its Persian name, *ancīr*, which corresponds to piercing and penetration. The fruits grow slowly, swelling from concavities at the root of the tree's broad leaves; as they swell, they begin to resemble breasts or testes, stirring seductive passions. As a consequence, the Pharisees gave it a name they chose for no other fruit they ate. This was because they peeled figs with an assiduous tugging, the same way they might have undressed a lover. Over time, it became shameful to be seen eating a fig in public, and even now from Iran to Anatolia, you can't simply go up to a grocer and brazenly ask for figs. They'll give you a dirty look and pretend not to have heard your request. The thing to do is to ask vaguely for "fruit," owning up to the fig in all its vulgarity, and eat it at home with your curtains closed. In any case, it's not as if you eat a fig slice by slice; you make out with it. You have to plunge your mouth into it, suck it out. Its red flesh is effervescent, animate, quivering. You can't do anything else until you finish eating the fig because it makes your fingertips so sticky. Perhaps this is why virgin girls and pregnant women weren't allowed near fig trees: so they would abstain from sex.

It also fell to the fig to remove fetuses from the wombs of women impregnated outside of marriage. This secret remedy was known only to midwives. They would stick a freshly cut shoot from a fig tree into the womb and poke around, causing a miscarriage. In those days, it was considered sorcery to pierce through the cervix and slough off the uterine membrane without killing the woman. As a consequence, the fig tree's creative and destructive power began to spread by word of mouth. They say that a woman who miscarries in this way must never again eat a fig, so she won't be poisoned by the dizzying taste of what she gave up.

Over those many millenia, I don't know whether the fig became more human, or whether we humans bent to the fig's temperament. Regardless, it began to speak every language in which its roots spread, to practice every religion that deemed it the tree of paradise. In due time, djinns settled at the foot of the fig tree, made it vengeful: it began contorting the faces and mouths of drunkards who peed on its roots at night, crippling children who tried to climb it, and spiriting away the memories of those who fell asleep in its shade. People revered and condemned the fig in equal parts, believing that this double-hearted androgyne had descended upon the world to dole out bite-size shares of the divine to all. The fig was a holy spirit that tamed humans even as it led them astray. It cultivated free will, inciting the ego; at the same time, it encouraged people to resemble one another, to become indiscernible, invisible. Strange that, in those times, the fig had two sexes. It seeded itself, spawned itself of itself, but it also acted as a devil hell-bent on driving humans out of paradise.

And so, while you were in the midst of the age of figs, you should have looked at Zevraki not with an eye toward history but with the eye of a barbarian who knows, deep down, that every civilization is impermanent, and with the hunger of a savage woman who, inspired by the cycle of the tree's life, has cultivated its spirit in her body.

In fact, I've never had the sense that you've fallen under the fig tree's spell, even once. You're just moved by the myths of the fig, that's all. Of course, the intimate bond you feel with Zevraki is important. But such bonds, such damnable attachments, all they've ever done is seclude the unique character of your spirit from the ineffable world. To tell you the truth, I still haven't figured out why you love figs the way you do. Have you ever even wandered through a street market to buy a kilo of figs? Have you popped a fig into your mouth in the middle of the crowd, licking the nectar that dribbles onto your lips? Tell me this first before you worship at the foot of the tree.

—

You're perched in your chair in the living room now, staring at Zevraki through empty eyes. Looking out upon its involuted branches, its sizable leaves, you're light as a ghost in search of a body. See the crystalline sky? You've never seen it from this angle, at this hour. The shadows that the leaves cast upon the earth seem to form new shapes altogether. Halcyon shadows, shifting with the light... You barely even realize the great lengths the fig branches have stretched in order to reach toward the sun. You're so lethargic compared to the tree. The history of your life has been extinguished by the faces in the photographs hanging on your walls. You're only now beginning to realize how vainly you've spent this life of yours, looking solely at people's faces.

Take that picture of the old man just across from you. He's sitting on the steps of a wooden house with a bay window, watching the passersby from behind a small counter displaying his homemade Muscat wines. You took this photograph in the village of Şirince, where you wandered the streets on an assignment for a magazine advertising vacation destinations. You were so thrilled when they published it as a full-page spread.

Do you think he's still alive? When you took the photograph, did you contemplate his mortality, his vulnerability? Weren't you implicated, the moment you pushed the shutter-release button, in the death of this man who made a living from his Muscat wine, in his subsumption into the relentless flow of time? Or rather, do you realize the extent of your implication? As I look at the photograph now, it's unclear to me that you took it yourself. You don't seem to have noticed the way he slumps to his left, or the large gem-set brooch pinned to the brim of his hat. If you had, you might have chosen a different angle, focusing your camera on something other than the labels of the wine bottles. Though you may not have noticed all the subtle details that illuminated his unique character at that moment, you nonetheless managed to capture them without realizing it. As such, you might be able to learn something by looking at your photographs, to recognize that it is the visceral that enchants the eye.

There are, moreover, some images that simply can't be captured. Bese's march toward Hızır, for example, her aloof demeanor when she returned, the dry grass stuck in her hair, the dubiousness of her affected solemnity: such moments are recorded only in an album of memory. Bese herself, and every moment concerning her, fades away with each passing day. As long as you continue to submit yourself to the world as it appears in your photographs, the world as it reveals itself to your eyes, any pursuit of Bese will fail. The brooch on the man's hat may have intimated absence, the absence of a woman, but that absence will never be able to conjure forth Bese's presence.

What you do is the art of twilight. The snapshots you take do not simply reveal the nostalgic time of photography itself: they foreground the tender absence that bleeds into each and every frame. At the very least, give me that absence from now on, that embryonic emptiness that finds its way into each and every shot you take. Because what rouses your being into presence is not your emotions but your emptiness.

—

Up till now, you've lived only by feeling, by remembering how you felt the day before, waiting patiently, alert to the feeling of something similar, something familiar, becoming your own carbon copy, a copy of the memory of your earlier feelings. The darkest aspect of your distorted memory must be your inability to understand why you wake up dead every single day. Even now, as I look at you, I can tell you can't bring yourself to weep. You refuse to shed tears whose source you don't recognize. Living is feeling… It's a beguiling notion, of course; it's concise, light, lets you fit in with others. But when feelings don't trigger rational thought, you can't do anything except feel them. So even if you don't wake up dead tomorrow, you'll become lifeless again the day after, acclimating yourself to the destructive banality of the way you feel now. With such a possibility on the table, my pretty-eyed girl, I beg you: weep. It's only a few days before you become your own corpse. Don't let go of this moment of reflection as you ache. Let it rouse your conscience.

Let us go into the garden, then, you and me, along with all the people we've pushed deep down inside ourselves, with our matriarchs who discovered wheat, our grandfathers who fell into traps, our midwives who were the finest of sorcerers, and with our murdered relatives. The shade has receded by now. Let's shiver to our bones in the spring's morning chill. The doves alight on the fig tree's branches, hunting among its leaves for spiders weaving webs. The stairs down to your garden are covered in bird shit, flies buzzing overhead. It's not really a garden, you're right, only a small space between apartment buildings. This narrow patch of grass only exists because they were never able to construct here, owing to the difference in elevation between the foundation of your apartment building and the ground. Zevraki doesn't dream of bearing fruit here. It lives on a plane of its own, this innocent creature isolated from humanity. Let's go sit beside it. There in your garden, overshadowed by buildings looming over us, laundry drying on back patios, old belongings wrapped in plastic, rolled-up carpets, skeins of yarn airing on balconies and tennis shoes on windowsills, piles of newspapers, empty flowerpots, overshadowed by so many other odds and ends, we'll recognize how desperately we struggle to impart our spirits into our possessions. Let's weep, together, let's cry out, remembering that we can't endure the invisible unless we look straight at it. Let's confess to the tree that these homes of ours, homes that ought to be torn down and demolished, and these bodies of ours, anchored to our homes, these domesticated, banal bodies of ours, are the only means we have to make ourselves visible. Let's leap out of this desolate time in which people aspire to perfection outside themselves, and into a time in which they attained perfection within. Let it be a time outside of time, before prophets cropped up and spoke plainly for everyone to understand, before any of God's commandments had been written down, before anyone except Gilgamesh had yet aspired to immortality. It doesn't seem we can sit still, so let's move together, as two letters side by side, a vowel and a consonant; let's become the syllable of an anguished cry.

I know of a person who found perfection within herself, at least for part of her life. At a time when the fig tree had existed for hardly two thousand years, a woman named Eliha lived at the foot of the Alborz mountains overlooking the Caspian Sea. Eliha had a well. It was a complete mystery as to how a woman had dug a well so deep, lining its walls with volcanic stones, all on her own no less. Some said she was strong enough to lift a ninety-kilo man with one arm; according to another rumor, the well had been dug by a slave whom she worked to the point of exhaustion. Some who claimed to have seen this slave from afar said he was an enormous man, big as an elephant; others who saw him from a little closer described him as a hunchback with a sagging chest; those who came close enough to see his face were stupefied, unable to say anything for sure. Nobody imagined that Eliha could have dug the hole in the earth herself, without hurry, slow and steady, even if it would have taken her months; nor did they conceive that she could have covered its walls with stones small enough to carry on her own. In fact, the task inspired in her a perseverance like marble. People would try to discern her age from the raven-dark hair that reached down to her ankles: some said she was thirty, some forty, others said she was ageless. Anyone with eyes would have recognized that she had been born to a roving tribe, and, that based on the scars on her face, her sunspots, the pockmarks on her chin, and her ossified nails, that she had reached the age of thirty. Her life story could be read in the bloodied whites of her eyes: waves wearing away at the stones of Oman, valleys filled with sunlight sharp enough to burn through skin, patches of fog that soak to the bone, freezing water in crater lakes, violent sandstorms in the desert, thick salt deposits that desiccate the soles. Eliha's olive-colored eyes really were bloody. Imagine: the wells of her eyes, bright red beads. In this strange woman's body were written the shifting climates of an enormous geography, and those who met her gaze were confronted by the split-second torment of death barely escaped; those who couldn't bear it would turn their heads the other way. It took quite a long time for people to get used to this solitary woman who lived hours away from the nearest village in a single-story house she had built herself, right next to an androgyne fig tree. She would usually appear in the market at the end of the summer, bartering a basket of her figs for salt and flour. She would say a few words in a shrill, caprine bleat before turning to make her slow departure home. The purple figs she left behind were enigmatic and enticing, becoming objects of lust in the village. Yet Eliha's perfection, borne of her ugliness, her solitude, and her silence, would only last until the night that Hızır *servant of servants* was planted in her womb.

—

Before I get to that night, I ought first to tell you about you Eliha's generosity. I already mentioned that she had a well; this well produced an extraordinary, foaming, pine-green water, slick as oil on the tongue. It truly had healing properties, most likely due to the minerals that seeped into it from the earth. Soldiers, migrants, traders, and wanderers would often stop at Eliha's well to rest on their way to Hazar. Its water would revitalize them immediately, would make them feel like they'd been reborn. You can more or less imagine how Eliha's mysterious reputation might have mingled with this water, which some described as an elixir of youth and others as the water of life. Together, the fig tree, the well, and Eliha formed a universe of their own, drawing passing travelers into their orbit like a black hole and wreaking havoc upon them before casting them out upon the distant horizon. But some men, particularly those who could stare unflinchingly into Eliha's bloodshot eyes, would forget for a moment where they had been going, choosing instead to stay by Eliha's side. Because Eliha was a woman who knew how to admire. Whomsoever she touched became second to none in her eyes. Her probing eyes might notice the way a thirsty soldier, smelling of death, his clothes caked in dried blood, hastily drank her water; or, perhaps, she might dwell on the deep scar on one man's neck, or the coil of hair twisted into a knot atop another's head. She would draw out those little details with words of affection. No man could tear himself away from this woman with bloodshot eyes that apprehended immediately the inimitable details of their bodies, and they consigned themselves to being swallowed up by her. Eliha would admire a scowl, or the pained expression of a callus; she adored the way that one man's shoulder might hang lower than the other, the way that a face changed when seen in profile. In her eyes, beauty lay in the body's natural lines, something that no peddler of cosmetics could ever hope to quantify or control. And so, men caught by Eliha's eyes could never easily peel themselves away from her bosom; gradually, day by day, they melted away, her meager legs fastening around their loins. Eliha slowly absorbed whomsoever she extended her hand toward, stripping them down

to the bones. These men would return to their home-
lands, miserable, utterly undone by the healing waters
they had imbibed. The legend of these waters spread
across an entire geography, enchanting and blighting
Eliha's reputation for searing affection. The well, the
fig, and the woman: they continued to underpin one
another, reaching as far as the ears of Melchisedek,
King of Salem.

You look like you've calmed down a bit. Your face has started to loosen up. Your irises are trembling, trying to bring Eliha to life in your mind. That's exactly the effect of these time-honored, ancient stories. They give root to all that has been and all that will be. This second, already passing, swells outward, becomes a colossal globe. Stories carve the pulse of time into sentences and line them up back to back, until that same pulse can be heard again and again. To tell a story is to fashion a shape out of time. In a way, to tell a story is to reorient the listener, to silence them... You are made to be quiet so you can listen, and you're cast into the time of Eliha, into a different space in which words grow ever larger. Eliha is a real woman, you know that. All I did was change her appearance a bit, to make her resemble the wounded and irascible Bese. I hope you don't begrudge me this kindness. After all, aren't you, Bese, and Eliha each held in thrall by the fig's wandering roots, as well as by Hızır's caprice? If kindness depends upon a docile steward then let me tell you this story, let me be your steward. Your passion for stories is, of course, borne of your existential suffering. That you might find solace in the imaginal realm they create. But look, I'm warning you, if you so much as try to write down what I'm telling you, driven by the desire to produce a masterpiece, if you hone my quaint voice and reconcile it with others', I'm telling you now, I won't forgive you!

At any rate, what difference will it make if you write this story, for goodness' sake? You might glue letter to letter, word to word, and thus fashion some inventive sentences; you might paint them in indelible ink, you might line up empty pages, spread them out and number them, but in the end, what effect would any of it have? Do you really think that the missing part of you will manifest itself in the form of a book? That puzzle you call the self cannot be made whole through objects made by handicraft or the creative mind. It's missing, it's always missing. And always so close. It's practically under your nose. Oh, if you could see me, if you could reach out to me... at the very least, you would feel like you'd touched your missing part.

—

Last night as you left your home you were someone else entirely. That alone is enough to make you a masterpiece. The torque and flux you experience living between two eras is far more unsettling than being the protagonist of a book. As soon as you arrived in

Ahırkapı, at the grounds of the Hıdrellez festival, you began to fade from the world. You fell far away from your body. Guarding your camera, you tried to find your way, jostling through the crowds. Those hundreds of people were huddled on top of one another, bellowing songs, dancing, drenched in sweat, and you were silent, grave as the stones in the sidewalk. Rocking in a cradle where death had been forgotten, a lurching, off-kilter motion. Everywhere you looked you were struck by their unhappiness, which verged on suffocation, a feeling papered over by the celebration of spring. They had found a way to distract themselves from that unhappiness, by inhaling one another's tepid, beer-scented breath. No matter whom you looked at through the viewfinder of your camera, all you saw were slaves to time, shackled to the future. They were jumping one by one over the big fire in the middle of the square, asking holy Hızır to grant their wishes. You never liked making wishes. To make wishes was to acknowledge what you lack. Perhaps because of your own enthusiasm for living a life of trepidation, you found the rush with which they scattered their expectations both reckless and inappropriate. Still, you couldn't stop yourself from watching all of this pageantry with interest. After they had leapt over the fire, some of the celebrants gathered down on the waterfront, to pour their unceasing desires into the sea.

I really don't like the way you stared at them so curiously. In fact, I've grown sick and tired of your hunger for learning, your flawed propensity to gird yourself with knowledge. I can't stand the coldness with which you scrutinized the crowd, the way you sneered, scornful of all those monotheists participating in this so-called pagan ritual. You flourished your camera melodramatically, as if to say, "I don't belong here, I'm just taking a quick look around." There was an old woman on the seaside taking pebbles from her pocket and casting them one by one into the Marmara, repeating to herself, "Take my grief and give me peace." You, cynic that you are, lazily counted the pebbles. You couldn't see her grief, only pebbles.

At the very least, don't do such things as you listen to me. On a day like this when I've devoted myself to you, before you've even left the house and cursed the world, before you've braced yourself for its cruelty, before you've anesthetized Bese's pain with the pain of others, let's draw your spirit out of the sack where it sleeps. I see your shame. That sterling pain you hide like a jewel in your belly: in this world, I'm the only one who knows of it. It blinds you, it draws you into its pitch-black void. You are somewhere between being and not being, in two places at once, like a leaf about to fall from its branch, ready to listen to everyone's stories. So, for now, stop dwelling on the roots of all those names I've given you; stop trying to find heroes their places in history. I'm not speaking in allegory here, I'm building a universe for you. Ever since you were born, I've been trying to figure out, word by word, just whose metaphor you are.

Melchisedek was disgusted by Eliha when he first saw her. In the time it took him to travel from the Kingdom of Salem to the Alborz Mountains, he had concocted a thousand fantasies, and had heard so much of her perfumed breath, her bloodshot gaze, the silken hair that fell to her ankles, that he hoped he would arrive to a woman whom he had known for a long time, rather than one he had in fact never seen. The Eliha that Melchisedek found, however, sprawled out on cushions in the shade of the fig tree, indifferent to the flies landing on her face, drooling as she slept, bore no resemblance to the woman of his dreams. The arch of her nose, the structure of her chin, the hollowness of her breastbone, told him that she was a migrant Pharisee. Greatly disappointed, Melchisedek crumpled to the ground. He fought off the urge to destroy this universe of lies, to destroy this well, this woman, this fig tree. When the snoring Eliha stirred from her sleep, she paid no heed to the copper-garbed stranger brooding beside her, as if out of spite. She scrutinized Melchisedek out of the corner of her eye before returning to her work with a disinterest that devastated him.

In Eliha's abode, the fact that Melchisedek was a

renowned king foretold by prophecy meant nothing whatsoever. That he was a sixth-generation son of Noah, by the line of Shem, was nothing to brag about before this diminutive woman. It was entirely inconsequential to Eliha that Melchisedek had close ties to Abraham; Abraham who had raised his head to the sky, Abraham who had dared to speak of his Creator in a time when the powerful strove to become gods themselves. It mattered not to her that Melchisedek received one-tenth of Abraham's spoils of war in return for his fidelity, enriching his kingdom with every passing day without having to spill any blood himself. He had embarked upon this long journey in order to write his own legend, but by the end of it, all his existential goals had fallen to pieces. He didn't know what to do except to freshen himself with the replenishing waters of Eliha's well. Her metallic coldness left him feeling forsaken. Eliha behaved as though Melchisedek wasn't even there, letting him have no more than two dried figs a day, brandishing her scythe to scare him off, hoping that he would leave as soon as possible.

To be honest, I'm not sure why he didn't. He probably wanted to learn to see himself through Eliha's eyes, or he simply grew too attached to her, like so many other men, addicted to the hellish friction between them. He waited for her for exactly twenty days. When he understood that Eliha would offer him no affection, he stripped stark naked and stood before her. Eliha looked and looked and looked at Melchisedek, but found nothing in him that she could love. He showed her the lines on his palms, the mole on the back of his neck, the birthmark hidden behind his ear, but still she took no interest in him. On the twenty-fifth night of his arrival, Melchisedek sprung on her and tried to force her legs apart. Eliha sank her teeth into his cheek and tore out a chunk of his flesh. Afterward, he beat her with a whip, but she didn't so much as whimper. When he burned down her home, she climbed onto a rock and howled like a dog until dawn. He erupted in rage, screaming at the top of his lungs. She mollified herself by gawking at him with her bloodshot eyes. On the fortieth day of his arrival, Melchisedek went hunting, unleashing his fury on his prey. Most often he would bring back a wild boar, but sometimes he returned with a dead cat or with rabbits, their heads dragging across the ground. Eliha never obliged him, refusing to eat a single bite of the meat. Each day that he was unable to possess her, Melchisedek was bewitched by Eliha's intransigence, beseeching Abraham's god to grant his desire. Eventually, on the ninetieth day of his arrival, realizing his tyranny would never work, he plucked a leaf from the fig tree, wrote Eliha's name on it in Aramaic, and left the leaf to dry in the sun. As it withered, a shape reminiscent of her began to form on its thick, veiny surface. Melchisedek sat himself down in front of Eliha and looked at the history the fig leaf told. He couldn't bear what he saw written there.

"You had goats," he said, "your brother herded the goats, and you had a camel-hair tent, and your mother stood at the threshold of the tent while your sisters frolicked in the poppy fields, and your father looked after all of you, and a bandit appeared before your father, a scimitar in his hand, blood dripping from the blade, and on the ground was your brother's severed head, you took the head into your lap, kissed your brother's eyes, your mouth covered in blood, and your father, he lost his son, his eyes filled with wrath, and he became crueler than the bandit, and rather than give his flock of goats to the bandit he snatched the scimitar from the bandit's hand and, just like that, killed your mother and your sisters, and when he couldn't find you he set the tent aflame, he tore the poppies from the earth in bloodcurdling rage, he searched for you but you hid behind the bandit, and the bandit was filled with shame, the scimitar in your father's hand, his eyes those of a man who had lost his world, you behind the bandit, and before him a father after his daughter's head, you took the enemy's hand and kept turning and turning to look back at your father, alone with his goats, he's still there, and you, turning back, you're stuck there, too, stuck, and you can't stop looking."

Melchisedek couldn't believe the words coming out of his mouth, and after listening to him, gravely, Eliha went away. She disappeared from sight like a small pebble tumbling down a cliffside. When she returned on the third day, her well had been stopped with a boulder and her fig tree chopped down at the base. Melchisedek was waiting for her, a docile bandit filled with shame. Eliha cut a shoot from the felled tree and placed it in a sack filled with soil. Then she held her hand out to Melchisedek, as if to say, come, take me. And so Melchisedek became everything that Eliha had lost. As they made their way toward Salem, she didn't look back, not even once.

No matter where she went, Eliha's true home was with her fig seedling. She carried that seedling from the Alborz Mountains to the shores of Hazar, from the Sea of Galilee to Phoenicia, all the way to Salem, where, as soon as she planted it in Melchisedek's garden, its roots continued their ceaseless march. They slithered under the ground, inch by inch, conquering sun-kissed stones near and far. Wherever it sprouted, it became the first protagonist of holy books. Wandering from the Mediterranean to the Aegean, from the Aegean to Thracia, it sprang up in the hearths of abandoned homes. In every place it grew, it set its roots deep in the hearts of the people there, who were overcome by the fig's ecstatic sweetness. It crossed the seas in the guts of swallows, mixing into new earth with the droppings. Sometimes it lacked the female sex, sometimes the male, and would be inseminated by pollen in the atmosphere. In any case, like Eliha and so many others, it too was displaced several times over. The very same fig eventually materialized like a lancet before Bese, in the hands of a surgeon who was about to test the pact between tree and human.

—

Immediately after Bese's abrupt departure to see Hızır, and her subsequent return, she and the forty exiles from Dersim continued on a painstaking twenty-day trek over the mountains of the Black Sea, eventually arriving at a village surrounded by tobacco fields, near Çarşamba. The flora and fauna there were new and unsettling, from the grass that grew on the land to the birds that flew across the sky. The villagers gave them roasted meat with corn bread, but the people of Dersim refused to bring the food to their lips, supposing the corn bread to be cooked cow dung and the meat to be unclean. After all the horrors they had endured, every place was fearsome and every person suspicious. In this foreign land, women wore their headscarves differently, the language was strange, the cuisine was peculiar, and they were unable to speak, unable to express what they knew about the art of honey, about the life-giving properties of walnuts. They began to swallow their language, word by word. But the legend of the cuckoo bird, a legend they brought from Dersim, stuck in their throats. This inexpressible story was one of regret, a morality tale about a boy who killed his sister and turned into a cuckoo. Through his song, cuc-koo, cuc-koo, he implored the universe for forgiveness. But because he only spoke the language of birds, he never found redemption, condemned to fly forever, incapable of ever landing.

And so the people of Dersim settled into a language they didn't understand, three to five families living in makeshift shacks without roofs, sharing the long and muted nights together. They huddled together when they saw the jackals come down from the mountains, believing them to be devils hell-bent on taking their lives. The villagers were offended, of course, that this handful of Alevis who came from Dersim didn't pray in the mosque and, instead, congregated for *cem* rituals out in the open, singing folk songs, and that the men and women leaned on each other and wept as they remembered their dead. Before long, the villagers began stoning the Alevis for their depravity. The people from Dersim quickly gathered their bedding and blankets and left Çarşamba for the city of Samsun, and when they were half a day's journey out, a military captain appeared before them. The captain told them they would not be allowed to enter the city and commanded them to go back where they came from, and so they set off yet again, on the four-day walk back to Çarşamba.

During this time, there was a change in Bese. Her eyes were brighter than they had been before, and her wounds were healing quickly. She didn't limp anymore, but carried herself with care, holding her groin. Recognizing the changes in Bese's posture, the women grabbed her by the arms and legs and laid her down on the ground. There was a midwife among them, esteemed for her skills as a surgeon, dexterous enough to remove a bullet stuck in the lungs, and just as she was about to insert a fig branch into Bese's cervix, Bese locked her legs together with all her might, yelling, "Don't! Don't ruin the fig for me!" She got to her feet and brushed her skirt with the back of her hands, refusing to let anyone violate the pact between her and the tree, and from that day forward they broke neither her spirit, nor the fig's.

The fig tree that crossed your grandmother's path that day wound its way from city to city, eventually springing up in a tiny garden behind an apartment building in Istanbul. And then you stood before it. Up until you met your Zevraki, your entire life had been no bigger than a kernel. And yet you claimed for yourself the power to dominate, and you tested that power on Zevraki. You called this tree Zevraki, annulling the name in which it had already taken root, like some mythic queen with the sovereign authority to bestow names. Whereas your grandmother, into whose hands you were born, protected you for exactly forty days from all the names that were rained down upon you, resisted all the commonplace names that your mother, father, aunts, and uncles impatiently thrust upon you. She searched your face for its true letters. On the fortieth night after your birth, you appeared in her dream *a girl graceful as a swan* and told her your name. Your grandmother awoke as if struck by divine revelation, leapt out of bed, took the bundle of you into her arms, and whispered into your ear the name you had given yourself. In her temperament, loving was a state of concentration that rendered every deed a masterpiece. She participated in the ritual of loving another being without compromising herself, and when she caressed your hair, she was also caressing your spirit. She knew in her bones that if you were loved, you would never be defeated.

And so, returning to Eliha… you can imagine how alienated she was from herself as the newest wife of the King of Salem. She passed her days under the canopy in Melchisedek's garden, where the fig she had planted slowly took root, listening to the sounds of all the people in the palace. Like a wild animal, she let no one near her, and she struggled to swallow all the overcooked foods she was offered. Among these people whose language she didn't understand, she availed herself of the wind, the stones cracking at noontime, and the rain. Eliha knew nobody there but Melchisedek, and after some time he grew bored of her. He would go into his other wives' rooms, eschewing her for weeks on end. When the fig tree began to bear fruit, Eliha revered it as her queen. Among the endless bloody wars fought over water and wheat, she had proven, through this tree, that she was alive. Using the milk of the unripe fruit to heal warts on people's hands, using salves made of its leaves to dry up pus-filled wounds, using its branches to end unwanted pregnancies: this was how Eliha's age of undoing had commenced. Because she had built a civilization out of the fig. She began talking more than she had before, and painted her eyes with black copper oxide, since she no longer had much use for seeing. No longer did she gaze admiringly upon men she liked, but turned her head away; she swathed herself in the sensuous scent of balsam, rubbing it all over her body and making people swoon. It didn't take long for her to embrace Melchisedek's religion. She poured out forty bowls of water every morning, thanking the heavens that she had been brought from the Alborz Mountains all the way to Salem, that she had all but forgotten the savageness of her previous life. She couldn't even recall her father's bloodshot eyes. With every passing day, the image of cruelty that had dominated her memory was fading, and evil became disembodied, a nebulous reality that had the potential to appear at any time and in any place. Evil had become an unknown. The only way for her to wield any control over her life was to become a mother, but not just any mother: she had to be the mother of an angel or a prophet, or at the very least a king—a child, that is, who could attain perfection beyond himself. And so she dreamed of a son.

There was nothing that Eliha didn't do to become pregnant with the right son at the right time. She ate snake eggs to boost her fertility; she climbed onto the roof naked on the nights of the full moon to let its light infuse her body; she soaked partridge meat in goat

milk at night, and gorged on it with sourdough bread
in the morning; when she made love to Melchisedek,
she lay on her back instead of getting on top, waited
for his warmth to flow into her; and when he came,
she turned onto her right side to direct his seed to her
right ovary. But still she couldn't conceive. With only
a few years left until menopause, she began offering
sacrifices regularly, making oblations to every god
she knew, kneeling twice before every idol she saw.
Finally, as a last resort, she tracked down a renowned
astronomer and knocked on his door. This scholar,
who hadn't seen the light of day for years, whose only
task in life was to observe the stars, who spent his
days dozing until the moon rose, was a pale, sallow,
frail man. When Eliha inquired after him, a woman
told her that he was asleep, and that she should return
after sunset. Eliha waited hours in the courtyard, but
as soon as the man awoke, he climbed up to the roof
and turned his head to the skies. He refused to receive
any guests. Day after day, Eliha came and went, but
had no luck meeting the astronomer. Finally, she was
struck by a nefarious idea. Bringing three slaves with
her from the palace, she set the scholar's home ablaze,
diving into the flames to rescue the man and his wife.
The scholar and his wife threw themselves at the feet
of this unsightly woman who had saved them from

the clutches of death. Newly without hearth and home, the couple gratefully accepted Eliha's invitation to Melchisedek's palace.

Once they settled there, however, the scholar's habits didn't change at all. He never left his room, preferring to sit on his balcony, astrolabe in hand, interpreting the shapes in the sky. Sleep became something of a poison to Eliha. She would wait in ambush in the corridors at night as the scholar wandered through the palace, and she would force open the doors to their room while they slept. Once, she even commanded one of her slaves to steal the scholar's journal, but she couldn't make sense of the strange characters or the geometric shapes he had drawn. Eliha had hoped this book of horoscopes would offer up a method, a prophetic revelation about the night, a sign for her from the sky. One evening, as the scholar and his wife ate dinner in their room, Eliha pressed her ear to the door and listened in. The scholar was explaining something to his wife. "Tonight," he said excitedly, "a star will appear in this position, southeast of the ninth star, and if we consummate when that star appears, you will give birth to an immortal son. But if we miss the birth of that star, this son of ours will never be born." Eliha went mad with joy upon hearing this. She immediately sent them a sherbet made from the milk of her figs to put them to sleep. Then she begged and pleaded with Melchisedek, eventually dragging him to her room with a relentless insistence. As soon as the long-awaited star grew bright, she grabbed Melchisedek by the waist and thrust him onto the bed, nearly swallowing his entire being with her sex. At first, he was confused and subdued, but Eliha was aflame with passion. She licked Melchisedek, caressed him, rubbed him forcefully, pulled at the hair on the nape of his neck as if demanding he become hard immediately. Sparks flashed in Melchisedek's eyes, and unsure whether it was pain or pleasure that he felt, he submitted to Eliha with a meekness unbefitting a king.

After that night, Melchisedek was bedridden for days, seemingly paralyzed. He had given everything to Eliha, from his kingdom to the marrow of his bones. The poor man didn't even have the energy to lift his arms. His senses and his strength revived only after he had eaten plenty of lamb stew, tray after tray of cinnamon pastries, and black Cyprus grapes by the bunch. Whereas the scholar and his wife, who woke to find that they had missed their star in the depths of sleep, beat their chests in grief, unaware that it was Eliha who had snatched away their son. The scholar had been waiting forty years for that star, and now had no choice but to wait for it to pass from one sign to another. Knowing that the second sign portended a son who would conquer the entire world, he offered his wife this consolatory piece of knowledge as he spread her legs, saying, "I'm giving you Zulqarnayn." And so Zulqarnayn and Hızır were implanted in their mothers' wombs under the very same star.

Countless millennia after the immortal Hızır was born to a mortal mother born of a mortal father, Bese was married to a wide-eyed young man in a hasty wedding before her belly began to show. Nobody had any idea what kind of child she was going to bear. The boy who emerged had floppy ears and slanted eyes, a whiny child who clung to his mother's skirt. His father called him Ali until he reached the age of two, then Kemal, then Mehmet when he turned six, and finally İlyas at fourteen. Naturally, the boy got confused. He was never sure of his place, had no idea how he should live under each new name. Thanks to his father's indecision, the boy's temperament never improved. Crying out of turn and quick to lose his temper, he became an unlovable child. Almost nobody remembers İlyas today, not even his siblings. When he was barely fifteen, he put on his father's shoes and went out one night, never to return. Even though the atmosphere at home drastically improved, Bese lost her mind over her son. There isn't a place in the Çarşamba Valley where she didn't search for him. Rumors circulated that İlyas worked as a porter in the Samsun harbor, that he had migrated to Tekirdağ and worked as a hireling on a farm, that he had fled to Istanbul and attended an art school there. Meanwhile, Bese saw his likeness in every passing young man, and couldn't stop herself from pursuing them. Almost every day since the family had migrated to Samsun unbeknownst to the state, she took to the streets in search of her son, looking in coffeehouses and tobacco factories, trade ships and barber shops.

In time, Bese found solace in the idea that İlyas might have passed into the next world, just as Hızır had been called into the sky, removed from the sight of mortal eyes, so that he might descend to earth at any time, wearing one of many faces in order to approach people as a friend. Perhaps her son İlyas had simply been a manifestation of Hızır; İlyas became for her an İlyas who contained Hızır. It's not that he had been erased from the earth; on the contrary, he had merely become invisible, had disappeared from sight. In this way, Bese gave up not on her son but on her eyes. Accepting that her lot in life was to yearn, she was ready to embrace all boys who were the same age as İlyas as if she had birthed each one herself. After the loss of her son, the distinction between water and steam grew sharper. İlyas's soul was water, his flesh the vapor that dissipated in the air above boiling cauldrons. She understood him to be a double-hearted being, just as iron melting in a fire is at once fire and iron. Though she never had the opportunity to watch her son grow, she held that double-hearted boy in her own singular heart.

It isn't all that surprising that your Zevraki doesn't bear fruit. It's as if the two of you have innate symmetry. When I look at you like this, from above, I can see you form a geometric whole, a curving shape that winds from you to Zevraki, and from Zevraki back to you. You are a spiral shell spinning in space, one the inner surface, mother-of-pearl, the other the calcareous outer surface, abandoned by the creature that inhabited you.

You always hoped in vain for Zevraki's fruit, as if a change in the tree would incite one in you. Every spring, you hired a horticulturalist to trim the roots; when fall came, you burned farm manure to spread around its trunk, and when that didn't work you poured liquid lime on its soil. Such attention multiplied the leaves on its eager branches, yet Zevraki has never given you a single fig. The loquat tree in the adjacent garden struggles to stay upright, so weighed down by its fruit, but Zevraki is devoted only to its leaves. What else can it do, waiting for a lacewinged bug nourished in the body of a male fig to come from afar and pollinate its female flowers? Zevraki has girded itself in patience for its fruit, resigned itself to the wild will of the fig wasp that will land on its flow-

ers who knows when. You are the one compelling
Zevraki to bear fruit, behaving as though the tree had
taken an oath to bear figs for you.

—

I know you. I've walked a long road with you, like a
god, an icon, nestled as a bloom in your breast. I have
roamed your capillaries, and in your body I've never
encountered even the slightest desire to give birth. It's
not that there's a problem in your bones, or that your
blood pressure is low, as it always is. You experience
time slowly. You absorb this slow temperament from
your poor circulation. When you fret, your stomach
releases excess acid: you're someone who wounds
herself from the inside. Your left ovary is more zeal-
ous than the right, perpetually preparing for the time
every month when your eggs mature and break asunder. Your uterine walls are supple and thin enough,
but your cervix doesn't open up to the world. The
discrepancy between your vagina and your cervix is a
dilemma for you, as if you've oriented that cavity in
another direction, the direction of darkness, perhaps.
In fact, it's almost as if you knowingly wished for this.
All it would take, if you did want to give birth, would
be a deft adjustment with your hand, but you choose
to leave your womb as it is. Perhaps because you so

resent having been born, you want to make sure that birthing another remains impossible.

Even at this age, you still haven't been able to impart any meaning to the word "child." As you evolved from a bony girl into a rounded woman, whenever the word came to mind it was always born as a stranger inside you. You were scared to death of developing an attachment to a stranger sullied into life by you. You don't know who they are, after all. Who would your child be, aside from another face in which to search for traces of your likeness, a body to dispense the essence of happiness, the host who bids you into the earth, the corpse for whom you've saved a space beside your grave? Sometimes you want children so that you won't die completely alone, until you remember that in giving birth to them you would also give birth to their death. Whenever you touch your empty groin, your hands feel a fire that burns eternal, and you snatch them away immediately. To multiply kin, to become someone's progenitor, seems a futile attempt to defy the world's impermanence. Doesn't giving birth, after all, mean reducing the integrity of your soul? You simply can't be sure.

—

Do you remember when you were five years old,

sitting on your mother's lap on the balcony of your house in Gelibolu, watching the passersby? You still didn't quite have a sense of heights, and you stood on her knees, hanging over the railing. Your mother's steady hands tugged lightly on your waist, making sure that you felt her strong, secure presence. That spring day, the branches of the acacia trees bent under the weight of their flowers, and an old woman passed slowly below you; a very old woman, her face wrinkled, the bones of her hands sharp and defined, her back hunched, unable to keep her balance, only able to walk by gripping the walls...

You asked your mother, "Was that granny born that way?"

Your mother replied with her usual talent for finding comforting and concrete answers. "Could such a thing be possible? When that granny was born she was a baby, then she grew as old as you, then she grew as old as me, then she grew as old as your grandmother, and finally she was as old as your grandmother's mother." You were horrified at these words and wept in squalls.

You were crying the tears of a god whose universe had been stolen away. It took hours to quieten you. The pain you felt wasn't rooted so much in your fear of growing up as in the fear that your mother would grow old. You didn't want to believe that her hair would grey, that her hands would become covered in liver spots, that she would shrink in her bed just like your great-grandmother, day by day, until she wasted away. The concept of a life span hadn't yet taken shape in your mind. From that day forth, you learned just what kind of thing life was from the bugs you crushed with rocks. When you began comparing your life with that of a tree, a rusty piece of iron, a butterfly, living came to mean freezing in place, lasting while you can. Immortality was a longing passed down from ancient times.

—

While we're on the topic, I should add that on evenings when you go on long walks in Yıldız Park, as the sun sets on the Bosphorus, painting the city gold, space buckles amid the beams of light filtering through the sycamore trees, and you and I walk in a different time altogether. We disappear at intersections and reappear on dirt roads, and you never even notice the change… But I watch the absence of you in all the paths you trace, watch your fingertips brush the heaving laurel branches, watch the algae's slow, cellular proliferation in the decorative fountain that you glance at in passing, and I, too, have died, again, and again, and come back to life.

Let's go through your first memory of Hızır, that unsettling night when you felt his breath on your skin. You were staying in Bese's stone house in Samsun, where your entire family sojourned every year for five to ten days, the ashure bubbling on the hearth, the tripe kebabs baking on an iron sheet. The fabled abode of flavors you would never taste anywhere else. You had just turned six. The streets were sticky, covered in the residue of the mulberries that had just begun to fall. Your fingertips were bright pink from collecting them all day. They put you to bed beside your grandmother. Buried there under her wool blankets, you breathed in the smell of lavender emanating from her white chest. The lavender smudged between her breasts, this old woman widowed at a young age, this mother of six children, gave you new insight into womanhood. You couldn't square the sexual sensations of that smell with the sexless body it came from. You were little, your curious eyes were enormous. You were the only one in your family not afraid of your grandmother, chasing her feet all day, asking her relentless questions. Every time she looked at you, her eyes welled up. Carrying so much love in that heart of hers, all by herself, was a struggle. That night, you

didn't blink as you watched her, awash in the moonlight streaming in from outside: this angry woman,
whose irascibility intimidated your entire extended
family, and who sulked even as she slept.

Just when you were about to fall asleep, you heard
sounds coming from the living room. Creaking
wooden floors, rhythmic footsteps drawing close and
receding, ceaselessly; someone was pacing in front of
the room where the two of you slept. You listened to
the footsteps for several minutes. You couldn't make
sense of the sounds, because you knew the rest of
your family members were asleep in their rooms on
the floor below. You stopped breathing out of fear.
You sat up in bed, listening carefully to the house,
drew the quilt over your face, trembling. Your grandmother was asleep, snoring loudly. You couldn't find
your voice, it had disappeared. All you could manage
to force out was a small croak, yet still the footsteps
continued. You curled up into a ball and covered
your ears, drenched in sweat beneath the quilt. Your
brain's thrumming, your grandmother's snoring, and
your own deep breathing coalesced into an unbearable cacophony. The footsteps pierced through that
cacophony, you felt them pacing in your head. A man
appeared in your mind, his body taking shape second
by second, and you saw his bushy hair, his leather

shoes, his tall, narrow legs, the shagreen leather vest on his back. You buried yourself in your grandmother's stomach, sobbing. She woke with a start.

"What's wrong, little one?" she asked, holding you tightly. That very instant, the sounds died away.

"There's a man," you said, stammering, "walking in the house."

Your grandmother looked curiously into your eyes. Her compassion was like velvet. Under the haunting glow of the moonlight she enveloped you in her soft, warm body. Night was a thick wall, practically without language. Even the bugs eating through the wooden beams didn't stir. Your grandmother couldn't hear anything in that silence. She smiled, combed back your sweaty hair, muttered a lengthy prayer and blew cool air on your face.

"Don't worry," she said, "I think Hızır must have come. I baked helva for him in remembrance of the spirits of our dead. He's just going to have a bite of that and leave."

There was no other remedy in that moment but to believe her. As far as you understood it, the person she mentioned was no more than an impertinent relative. By the time you finally fell asleep, exhausted, Hızır had planted himself in your mind.

Over the following days you pestered your grandmother about Hızır. You learned that he was an immortal who recognized God's good servants by bringing plentitude into their homes, that he came to people's aid in difficult times, that he appeared suddenly and disappeared just as suddenly, that he could appear before you at any moment in the least expected way. He was a resplendent being who would live until the apocalypse, the only immortal who dwells in the imaginal realm between worldly life and the afterlife, who knows the secrets of time and space. Your grandmother spent hours telling you about Hızır, but she never told you anything more than this. Nor did she grow weary of repeating those same sentences, over and over, each time as if they held new information. One day, she fixed her black eyes on yours and told you she would reveal to you the greatest secret of all, but that if you related this secret to anyone, the world would be lain waste, and she made you swear on the dead bodies of your mother, your father, and your siblings. So you did. You quickly swore on their dead bodies, and she brought you to a storeroom, where pickle jars, marmalade pots, coils of sausages, winter melons, canisters of oil, and canvas sacks big and small, were all neatly organized.

"Look," she said, "this is our Hızır pantry. Whatever I take out of here, the same thing appears in its place. Whenever something is removed from this pantry, even a single grain of rice, the Prophet Hızır comes and replaces it." You didn't believe this story in the slightest, but you wanted to so badly. Having grown up in a home ruled by the language of reason, the mystery of Hızır got under your skin. For the rest of that summer, you kept watch for Hızır day and night. You couldn't say anything to anyone because you had taken such a grave oath, so you had no way to explain to your mother why you were loitering so suspiciously in front of the pantry. According to your grandmother, Hızır could appear to you in different guises, sometimes as a beggar, sometimes as a rich man, sometimes as an orphaned child, sometimes as a laborer. Sometimes he was light-skinned, sometimes dark. The only way you could tell that he was Hızır was by grabbing his thumb, because he didn't have a bone there, no matter his guise. Those who managed to grab hold of Hızır's thumb won his friendship for a lifetime.

—

The day you were born, your grandmother planted a fig tree in her garden. That tree was your secret sibling; there was always a wooden divan underneath it. On summer nights you would lie on the divan, looking up through the leaves at the stars. Years had passed since the incident with Hızır; you and the fig were both fourteen years old, and you had long since forgotten the vow you had once made. You were fond of your physics and math classes, astonished when you learned that the stars in the sky had been alive millions of years ago. You felt a twinge of grief because you had no way of knowing which era of history coincided with the starlight traveling through space. Perhaps there, beneath the fig tree, you were looking up at light from the Pleistocene.

At the same time, you couldn't stop thinking about the boys you'd been chasing. Your breasts ached, your armpits itched. You were overcome by your thirst for those boys, and pleasure inflected your shame at being attracted to their deepening voices, their sharpening features, the bitter smell of their sweat filling the air around them. As a child, you were only abstractly aware of what was above the waist. But as you grew, you came alive lower down. The widening of your pelvis made you understand how your bones, your body, was developing. In the caresses you exchanged with other girls, you learned how to let your legs and belly be free. On one of those same, abundantly starry summer nights, as you roamed somewhere between your body and the world, a miserable-looking old man limped into the garden behind you, hauling a sack of tin cans. The clanging and clanking grew louder as he approached you. He must have been one of those destitute people who gathered cans to sell to the scrap dealer. "We don't have any cans," you said as he approached. But he continued walking toward you, paying no heed to your words. He stopped in front of you, letting the sack clatter to the ground.

"I'm hungry," he said.

You gawked at him. He hadn't begged; he had made an outright order. Unsure how to respond, you ran to your grandmother. When you told her that a bedraggled man had entered the garden, she was bowled over. She hurriedly filled a tray with meat and beans, yogurt, stewed fruit, and rice. There was a reverence about her that you had never witnessed before.

She wouldn't let him see the palms of her hands, and she kept her eyes on the ground, her head down, stone-silent as she put the tray down before him. You sat on the stairs, never once taking your eyes off the man in the garden. Despite your grandmother's multiple reprimands, you stubbornly refused to budge. He paid no heed to the fact that he was being watched as he devoured the food, a dour expression on his face. Upon finishing the last morsel of his meal, he produced a filterless cigarette from his jacket pocket and puffed on it complacently. You were angry. His lack of gratitude seemed to you a sign of his shamelessness. He didn't even offer any thanks as he turned to leave. Later when your grandmother washed the dishes, you asked who that rude beggar was.

"It was the Prophet Hızır," she said.

Her response cast you out of that first garden with the fig tree, out of her miraculous pantry. You hugged her tenderly, your smile bittersweet. It crushed you to see her treat beggars like prophets.

The fact that Hızır and Zulqarnayn were planted in their mothers' wombs under the same star must have bound them to one another: the two were like fraternal twins whenever they were together. One was a celestial personage who took possession of his mother Eliha's fate by ensnaring it; the other was a world conqueror whom his father disparaged to no end. Hızır was a son his mother tore out of herself by force; Zulqarnayn, a son his father conjured up. One was conceived the moment the fated star appeared; the other, after it had traced a bow in the sky. That they both found life under different horoscopes of the same star meant that while Hızır and Zulqarnayn began life as companions, over time an insurmountable distance sprung up between them.

Zulqarnayn you know already; he's a familiar figure. He bears resemblance to Suleiman the Magnificent, Alexander the Great, and Mehmet the Conqueror, along with other rulers who set their sights on amassing the world. He was a monstrous warrior, seething with dreams of lands he could conquer, formidable as a jet-black bull with two horns protruding from his forehead. Hızır, conversely, was an introvert; his mother died giving birth to him, and as a boy he would sit along seashores and lose himself in contemplation. He was fond of flower seeds and tree roots, and he admired the cycles of the soil. Next to his milk brother Zulqarnayn, who girded himself with a sword and learned the art of fighting at an early age, Hızır was nonchalant, puny.

The trick that Hızır's mother had played was written into his flesh. To him, the missing bone in his thumb was not so much a distinction that marked his privilege as an augur that he might one day lose all his bones. He had startling notions about how he might be able to die without experiencing death. In order to pass the threshold to eternity, he thought, he had to vanish out of life itself.

What's more, he was ugly. The prepossessing ugliness that he had inherited from Eliha seemed to contribute to his fame, and as such, he saw it as something to be purged. Zulqarnayn wrestled with worthy adversaries in city squares, but Hızır took no relish in such spectacles and instead sought refuge in the mountains. He never gorged himself, never drank more than a couple sips of water, ate as little meat as possible, and spent entire days chewing on grape leaves when he could find nothing else, offering his gratitude to the invisible god of Abraham. By disavowing ambition in favor of contemplation, he vowed to rid himself of the flesh.

—

Melchisedek was utterly displeased by his son's behavior. He saw Hızır's tendency to spirit himself away as disobedience to his own authority, insolence that disparaged his rule, and most importantly, a fundamental lack of respect for his rights as a father. He stopped at nothing in his efforts to try and curb his heir's ascetic lifestyle. Wherever Hızır went, Melchisedek would send his men to bring him back. Even when Hızır had hidden in caves, tree stumps, or shepherd lodges, they would storm in and destroy those silent sanctuaries; they would get him drunk and force women on him in vain attempts to make him indulge the pleasures of the flesh and stir his tranquil blood. Little did they know, Hızır had been intoxicated since birth, his head filled with smoke, his words few, his eyes so narrow they let almost no light in. He was sick and tired of his body and he didn't want it anymore. For this reason, he never succumbed to the women winding around him or the wine saturating his palate.

And so various rumors about Hızır began circulating, comparing him to the enigmatic prophet Idris. Idris, who never died, whose existence remained an enduring mystery, was an enlightened man whose

eyes were so sharp he could count in one glance all
the leaves on a tree; he was powerful enough to make
clouds talk, renowned for his unerring powers of divination, and crowned with the three great blessings
of prophecy, wisdom, and the sultanate. He was the
first person to take up a pen and write in letters, after
a mere four meetings with a pockmarked stranger
regarded by some as a djinn and others as an angel.
Based on these meetings, he wrote a book of revela-
tions that amounted to thirty pages. Though he was
silver-tongued in seventy-two languages, he was unable to impart a single sentence of that book unto the
seventy-two tribes of Babylon. Unable to convince
anyone of his prophecy, he withdrew, sulking, and
took up tailoring. With a deftness of hand inherited
from his mother Baraka, inventor of the needle, he
began to manifest the likeness of cloth to body. The
same sentence always poured from his mouth as he
stitched: "From my position I have seen both heaven
and hell." The day Idris no longer found solace in this
incantation, he disappeared, leaving behind neither
footprint nor bloodstain, and was never heard from
again.

An age after Idris disappeared from this world,
he was revived in the countenance of Hızır, in part
due to Hızır's own eccentricity. Day by day, Hızır

was becoming the spitting image of Idris. Like Idris, he too would wander off quietly, returning with an unsettlingly cheery expression, as if he'd discovered all the secrets of the world. "He knows something, but what?" Melchisedek grew more and more resentful at his own powerlessness, unable to wrap his hands around whatever it was that his son knew. Helpless, he put Hızır in chains. For months, he tried to break his son's patience, giving him no more than a bowl of water and two slices of bread every day. But Hızır was content in the dark between four walls, contemplating the layers of the sky and the entrails of the earth. Melchisedek, on the verge of exploding from frustration, had his son whipped forty times every day until his skin was raw. Consequently, Hızır began to measure everything in the world using the number forty. It seemed to him that anything multiplied by forty was equal to one, such that forty levels of pain were reduced to one, forty days became one, and forty thousand breaths were only a thousand; and so with every passing day, time grew more potent for him. When Melchisedek gave up hope on reforming Hızır and allowed his son to emerge from his cell, Hızır's eyes were not blinded by the light of day.

—

Zulqarnayn waited to receive Hızır. His eyes were sharp as daggers, converging formidably with the horns on his forehead. With the gaze of a half-god, half-beast creature, he regarded the peoples who faced his sword with contempt. Since last they had seen each other, the veins on his neck had grown even thicker. Hızır stood, skin and bone, before Zulqarnayn, who was imperious as a colossal statue and whose zeal had all but cast him in bronze. His army of five hundred men stood behind him, half of them archers and half cannoneers, rendering him a memorial of himself. Zulqarnayn dwelled endlessly on the places he would conquer, the castles he would erect on hilltops, the iron wall he would build to keep out the nations of Gog and Magog who were bent on wreaking havoc on the world. But there was one thing Zulqarnayn did fear: death. Whenever he suffered a wound he was plunged into existential horror, confronted with his body's fragility. He would shudder when he found lice in his hair, panic when his stomach ached, cringe when dust caused his eyes to water. And everything he'd heard about the land of the dead chilled his blood. That was why he wanted to attain immortality before he conquered the world. He needed to discover the enchanted water of life, that object of poets' songs, its location found only on maps drawn by sorcerers in trances, and which Gilgamesh searched for and never found. Zulqarnayn had no choice but to find this water, trickling out from underneath a jade stone in a far-off place, mentioned in a codex left to him by his father.

"Come, brother," Zulqarnayn said, grabbing Hızır by the shoulders, "let's leave this place."

"Of course," Hızır replied, his tone carefree and light as a feather blowing in the wind, an expression of erudite maturity on his face.

As Hızır and Zulqarnayn left the city, their mighty army raising a cloud of dust, they encountered the Prophet Abraham on his way to Mount Moriah to sacrifice his son. In one hand, Abraham held the reins of his donkey, its back loaded with firewood; in the other, he held the hand of his son Isaac, whom he loved more than life itself. Abraham's face bore a determined, grievous expression. Isaac trembled like a leaf next to his executioner, the terror of the sacrificial offering glinting in his eyes. His complexion was pale and waxen, having been afflicted by nightmares ever since he was a baby. As a son who was about to be sacrificed to reward the faith of his father in a test of that very faith, Isaac envied Abraham's devotion to God. Hızır stroked the boy's head, hoping to give him strength. Isaac took two steps back. The

Prophet Abraham released Isaac's hand to embrace Zulqarnayn, warmly wishing him godspeed. From that day forward, history has always been told from the same beginning, that of the intimacy of conquerors and prophets. Whenever conquerors and prophets cross paths, nobody ever mentions the Isaacs.

Imagine an army. Soldiers garbed in hides and pelts, spilling blood everywhere they go. They've aged over the course of their travels, and as they've aged, they've begun to resemble not their fathers, but one another. Since leaving their homes, most have lost their teeth. They've left bastard children in their wake, to be born on the threshing floors of the villages they burned and destroyed, accustoming the world to this state of abandon. The wounds they've suffered have left them drastically altered. Blind, maimed, crippled, each is a specter garbed in the spoils of war as they lumber eastward in one large mass like an enormous bleeding beast. They haven't just spilled blood in their search for the water of life; they've also tasted all the earth's elements, drinking water from every river they conquered, from every crater lake and spring they've encircled. In the midst of two pillages and a massacre, they learned the difference between the taste of sulfur and that of sodium, and then they made their way toward the netherworld to taste magnesium. These men have resolved the mystery of stone, discovered the components of nature, the many different kinds of water on the face of the earth, and attained all this intricate knowledge only by disemboweling and decimating the many peoples they encountered. With every step they've taken, they've ushered suffering into the world, afflicting people with the black plague, and with so many other scourges.

Eventually, the strange men in this army no longer pay heed to which waters they drank, nor to the solitary wanderers who happened upon them, accompanied by leaden storms. They pay no heed to the bard whose sole task in life was to pluck living words out of the air where they originated, nor to the wandering saint who owned only his staff, nor to the carpenter dedicated to deciphering the temperament of the sycamore trees, nor to the vagabonds seeking the borders of kingdoms, nor to the shaman in eagle-owl feathers who took flight toward the pure core of the universe. They stop caring about the water of life trickling out from under a delphic stone, believing that spiritual wellspring was fated for Zulqarnayn, and Zulqarnayn alone. Zulqarnayn, however, the image of stateliness atop his raven-dark horse as he led his army, still has no idea that it is Hızır, riding on a gray horse right behind him, who will be the only one destined to drink the water of life.

Do you think Zulqarnayn was deceived, or simply mistaken? Or maybe he was imprisoned by the legend of heroism attributed to his name before his birth?

Perhaps he was just a rather ordinary person shackled to the Zulqarnayn who appeared in his dreams, his antlers fully developed and his black beard falling in ringlets upon his chest, doomed to wage endless wars, risking his own ruin through his desire for eternal life. Perhaps the fact of the matter was that he wanted nothing more than to wrestle and to hunt quail. Perhaps he had long since stumbled upon the eternal without realizing he had done so.

—

Your grandmother once told you a tale about Zulqarnayn, do you remember? The one where he and his fearless army made their way toward the land of cruelty where the sun never rises? He stopped at the door of a large palace and knocked three times.

A rumbling voice rose up behind the door. "Who are you?"

"I am Zulqarnayn!"

The palace's iron-framed wooden door creaked open slowly. Your eyes grew wide with wonder. You held your breath. You could hear the rusty hinges of the door, tearing through the silence.

A figure appeared, wearing a white shirt, his face the color of lilies. He looked witheringly into Zulqarnayn's eyes and said, "O Zulqarnayn, are the lands you've conquered not enough, that you've come to knock on my door?"

Zulqarnayn held out his empty palms. "I have no possessions. I distribute all my spoils among my soldiers."

"Armageddon approaches. Had you possessions, they would be worthless," the young man said. "I am Israfil, master of the ramparts. When I receive the command to blow my trumpet, all will hear its sound, and the last judgment will be held in this place." Then, as he took something resembling a stone from his pocket, he instructed, "Take this and measure yourself."

At this point in the story, you thought about all the stones you'd gathered from beaches and hillsides. You didn't know yet quite why you loved stones. I think you saw in their spirit-shrouded surfaces something inscrutable and immaculate. Mathematically immaculate... Once, wandering the pine forest in Sarıkamış, you found a piece of obsidian; I remember it like it was yesterday, that stone seemed to you a shard cleaved from a jet-black planet, its surface glimmering brightly. You were convinced that it hadn't come out of the ground but had fallen to the earth, that you could give life to this piece of raw, unhewn matter by blowing a part of your spirit onto it.

The stone Israfil gave to Zulqarnayn felt incredibly light to him. For days he passed it back and forth between his left and his right hands, trying to estimate its weight. He carried it in his casque, pressed it against his chest, held it in his pockets; he rubbed it between his palms to warm it, observing how long it took to cool afterward; he compared the shape of the stone to his heel, his shoulder, his kneecap; and when he couldn't find the ratio between himself and the stone, he compared it to other stones.

Measuring stone against stone was without a doubt the greatest stalemate Zulqarnayn ever faced. Just think: one granite, the other quartz; one marble, the other amethyst; one round, the other rectangular; one rough, the other smooth; such that he couldn't compare stones at all, and even if he were to find one stone equal to another he would have to obsess over each, looking at one in order to understand what secrets it could reveal about the other.

Eventually, Zulqarnayn realized the impossibility of this task, and began comparing not the stones themselves but their weights. Even you, with your grandmother's honeyed voice holding you rapt, more or less predicted at this point that Israfil's stone would weigh more than any other that existed in the world. And that's just what happened. Even when he presented his scales with the heaviest stones he could find, the stone Israfil gave Zulqarnayn was always heavier. Zulqarnayn was exhausted, defeated, like a commander who'd never won a single battle. Though he had taken on so many dozens of armies, won hundreds of wars, he couldn't solve the mystery of this singular stone.

That which you call a heart is a bottomless reservoir, a dark chasm that cannot be apprehended with reason, where any attempt to do so will cause you to lose your balance, to be sucked into an endless whirlpool. When Zulqarnayn entered that dark chamber and saw himself on earth, toying with a rock, he finally realized what a sorry state he was in. He felt as though he'd wasted an endless amount of time on that stone. With no escape in sight, he beseeched Hızır: "Save me, brother, I beg you," appealing to his milk brother to help him liberate all the parts of his self with which he had imbued the stone. Hızır took the stone from Zulqarnayn and, with his typical air of extraordinary tranquility, held it in the air, up against the light, and looked at it for a long time, as though he could see something inside it. You squinted your eyes at that moment. Every word that poured out of your grandmother's mouth was building itself a home on your face. You lived in the time of the story, in a different reality. You experienced its plot as if remembering something you yourself had experienced, long, long ago. All of it unfolded in the crucible of your witnessing. Hızır placed Zulqarnayn's stone in one plate of the scales, and in the other he put a handful of earth, letting the scales demonstrate the equilibrium between the two. Zulqarnayn had never expected such a simple solution. Its sheer simplicity was a blinding light that exposed the mediocrity of his own thought, the disgrace of all the time he had wasted.

"Fine," Zulqarnayn said, "but how did you know to measure the stone against earth? Explain yourself!"

Hızır tossed Israfil's stone to the ground and threw his arm around his milk brother's shoulder. "I don't know how I knew, but when I saw the stone I remembered something I already knew."

Zulqarnayn wasn't convinced. "So was that the mystery of the stone, then? That it weighs as much as a handful of earth?"

Hızır was offended. "Don't you understand? The significance of the stone isn't its weight. The stone represents the closeness and distance between us. It is the means to measure you against me, me against you."

Such stones speak louder than humans sometimes. Think of the many monoliths erected to point to the gods' meeting places; the border stones; the gravestones; the stone of Bethel that Jacob first used as a pillow, before building a pillar upon it that served as an entrance to heaven; the sacred stones polished to a shine by the ancestors of the Shona people in Zimbabwe; the Black Stone in the Kaaba; the marble of sacrificial altars; the fallen meteors and the temples built around them: they infect people with the tarnished feeling of having encountered the infinite.

When you touch stones, I am cooled; a refreshing inebriation spreads through me. Stones, whether from beaches, riverbeds, or hillsides, let you fathom the possibility of becoming one with the universe. Because a stone is a different kind of thing. It is an outsider. It shows no sign of its inner will. An enormous boulder can be made into a monument by humankind, yet it is never anything more than what it already is: plain rock. And yet, thanks to that rock, the reverberations of humankind resound across space and time.

What I mean to say is that as your grandmother told her story, you grew closer to stone. You touched pebbles, agate, quartz, granite with veins of gold, all those stones that measure one person against another. So when your grandmother continued her story, describing a broad and endless prairie, you saw the scene unfold before you. A white light spread across the horizon. The earth had turned red with autumn, and great tangles of brambles caught the wind, tumbling across the prairie. Zulqarnayn was secretly annoyed with Hızır. He had spent a long time puzzling over Hızır's words, trying to comprehend them, but he simply couldn't find within himself what sense there was in using a stone to measure one person against another. Because, in fact, to know something is to find its sense within oneself. So Zulqarnayn endowed stones with a different meaning, one that Hızır could never know, to make it seem that he had found this knowledge within himself. When he and his army arrived at this flat, expansive prairie, he turned to his soldiers and gave them a cryptic command.

"Go and gather as many stones as you desire! But no matter how many stones you gather, you will regret it."

As the soldiers laid down their weapons and began searching the prairie for stones, your grandmother surprised you with an unexpected question: "If you had been there, how many stones would you have gathered?"

You shrugged your shoulders and replied without thinking too much about it. "I don't know, probably just one."

When the soldiers returned to Zulqarnayn, every single one of the stones they'd gathered turned to gold. Now, your face bore an expression of deep resentment. You couldn't hide your disappointment. Your grandmother asked you, "Do you regret your decision?" Unable to reply, you swallowed the feeling of loss.

After you heard the tale of Zulqarnayn, you clutched your stones every night when you went to sleep. As you slept, you appeared to me a diaphanous globe, shrouded in your own spirit, almost as if sleeping with the stone bound you to some sense of infinitude. What I don't know is whether the stone in your hand represents earth or gold, and I still wonder which one of the two you cling to.

It's almost noon. Your face is beginning to pale with hunger. At least have a sip of water. Fry an egg, brew some tea, do something, I really resent how you don't feel your own hunger. You're half dead in your seat, it just won't do! And you still haven't gotten dressed; your hands and feet are ice-cold. How many times has the phone rung, and yet you haven't moved a muscle? Strange things come to my mind as you sit there motionless in your chair. It's almost as if you feel like you're being watched from outside, striking a pose for whoever might be looking. You are the focus of an eye wide with curiosity. Or else, are you looking at someone wandering barefoot in your garden? Are you imagining yourself there, your feet feeling the lingering moisture from yesterday's downpour, watching it turn to vapor in the noontime heat? Are your eyes dazzled by the tiny floods of light cascading down from the rooftops, have you joined the nation of colors and shapes, have you become a colony of spirits? Is this how you hope to heal? By touching things with the substitute of a substitute of a substitute? Are you going to split yourself apart for the hungry, the poor, the aggrieved, the happy spirits haunting the streets? Your shadow has become the refuge of a large, hud-

dled crowd, and who else will you fasten that shadow
to except yourself, watching the garden from where
you sit? For goodness' sake, please give up this zeal
for plurality, now is not the time. Right now, there is
only you and me. We are the victims of an affliction
that measures you against me, me against you. We
have only each other to talk to. Even if you looked
into the eyes of that version of yourself, the one who's
out there right now in your garden, observing the
cockleburs bursting through their sheaths, you still
wouldn't feel her curiosity in your heart. The seconds
between you are centuries long.

I understand why you do this; really, I do. As a
child, whenever you wanted to escape from a given
situation, you would imagine yourself a little ways off,
occupied by something quite different. That other self
of yours was a willed hallucination. You never could
have imagined that such an apparition could have
been imagining you in return. To imagine… what a
fantastic thing, what an enchanting thought, to accept
at the same moment the possibility that something
is or is not, and to believe more strongly in the *or*.
Whatever you imagine, you bring into reality. If you
want illusions more truthful than the woman in your
garden, have the courage to turn your face to me. See
at last who the mutterings in your head belong to.

Find me among the mottled shadows cast by the rays of light filtering into your home. Look into my eyes, dim with fear. Let me tell you everything you have imagined.

While we're on the topic of your imaginings, I want to remind you of the day you went fishing, that cold winter morning when you and your university classmates went to Kızılırmak River. The hazy weather had been the only reason you wanted to get away from Ankara. You didn't know a thing about fishing, but you wanted to fit in with your friends, and so, as the mist of the waters struck the stone you were sitting upon, you cast your line into the Kızılırmak and considered what it meant to lure a fish. A fishing lure is truly a strange thing. Fishing, after all, depends upon deceit. Only humans could have concocted the deceit of bloodying the bait on a hook to catch a fish, so you figured that, in the encounter, either the fish on the hook would become somewhat human or the human would take on some qualities of the fish. Your friends, of course, paid no mind to your absurd ideas. They found your thoughts "feminine" and "antiquated." At a time when colonialism was retrenching its hold on the world, they said, positing a common consciousness between animals and humans was nothing more than a petit bourgeois dalliance, an exercise in pointless, pseudo-philosophy. "Don't presume so quickly," you said timidly, and then closed your mouth. You didn't say another word to them until you got home. Nonetheless, when the line grew taut in your hands, you threw yourself backward in excitement, trying to hook that fish, and in that moment a mortal bond formed between it and you. They say that a hooked catfish stares at its captor as it dies, and that fish really did look you dead in the eyes. You struggled to hold on to its slippery body, practically fighting the fish to remove the hook's barb. You could see its vital force. Amid its thrashing you could hear its gentle pain; it gave you a pleasure that you had never felt before. It was erotic, and faintly nauseating. The fish's helpless writhing intensified, its gills opening and closing wildly, its moment of death immanent yet unknowable. Rather than tossing the fish into the bucket, you held it in your hands, watching it with cruel interest for several minutes, until your fellowship in death came to a sudden end. The fact that this catfish could be killed so easily, a fish whose size meant it must have produced at least three generations of eggs, gave you the authority to issue such a verdict. Your hands were like steel, your spine rigid. The animal opened and closed its mouth, trying desperately to breathe in the empty air, and you fancied yourself a cruel god overseeing some monumental tragedy, feigning sorrow over a death that was not your own. The only thing left of the fish's travail was the lure that had served to catch it, a testament to humanity's deceit. You tried to use your penance to complete those unknown parts of yourself.

This story has its flipside as well, the story of the dead fish coming to life…

I don't know why, but as I recount this, I find myself exchanging future for past: I find myself in the imaginary time of an ancient country where strange birds sunder the clouds. Yoked by the tales I've tied together, end to end, vaulting from now to then, from then to now, I keep circling around you. I am weaving you a memory. If a fish is going to be brought back to life, even if only through the deftness of words, it is because I can see, when I look at your hands trembling in your lap, how that newly resurrected fish thrashes in the water. Every move you make cracks open the husk of a memory hidden inside me. I have no way of knowing if it is I who is recounting or you who are making me speak, no way of knowing which of us guards the memory of these stories.

As I look at you, I see a group of hunchbacked men emerging from fog, exhausted, bloodied, on horseback: Zulqarnayn's army. There must have been no more than forty of them left. Their hair had gone white. Every night, they took shelter in caves, sleeping with their faces turned toward the moon, hoping its light would fend off their mortal nightmares.

Whenever a horse whinnied with unease, the men found shared solace in the crackling fire. This was why they smelled so strongly of soot. Since the slightest rustling of the grass interrupted their dreams, their sleepless, weary eyes stared off into the distance. They had grown tired of the forests' unknowability, of the deserts' blinding brightness. Though they continued to cross mountains and seas, they had given up hope of finding the elusive water that bestowed immortality. Each of them avoided their companions' gaze, not wanting to encounter in another's eyes the same dread afflicting their own mind. When by chance their eyes met, shame filled the air like flashes in the night. They didn't want to remember the times when they shared their disgusting rations, back when they still had food. They had grown tired of one another's barbarism. All they had left of their hymns of glory, honor, and bravery were their splintered bodies, their missing eyes, their torn ears, their shorn fingers. They no longer even felt the need to mourn their dead comrades. Recalling the sheer number of those stricken with fever from drinking the waters of rotting cisterns, those left behind in the agonizing grip of gangrene, those who were executed for rebelling, they were grateful to call themselves alive. But the distance between them and life had become so insurmountable that it was as if they girded their spirits and what remained of their bodies in loss. They limped toward an unknown destination with the caustic silence of a funeral procession, surrendered to the horses' instincts, undaunted by the stark white peonies, or by the strange cries that echoed out of the depths of the spruce groves, or by the iridescent scavengers that appeared and disappeared as if out of tales of hell, as they made their way to the end of the world... I'm looking and looking, and I can't find you there. You haven't entered their ranks. Nor are you a prisoner being drawn along behind a grey horse. No, you are the entire scene itself: you are all of the long-suffering soldiers climbing this tall mountain in China, you are the water droplets in the milky fog, you are the trees whose leaves resemble golden coins. You are perhaps the only conscience that truly wants the water of life, and that sordid army is the measure of your proximity to its source.

There was a profound agony on Zulqarnayn's face. A young Mongol's lance had left a deep wound on his side that just wouldn't heal, the noxious infection rotting its way deeper into his body with every passing day. He barely had the strength to hold up his head to bear the weight of his three-spiraled horns, which had become infamous far and wide. After the dozens of nations he had brought to their knees, after all the strongholds he had conquered, and the soldiers he had slaughtered, it seemed so meaningless now to either conquer or be conquered. Yet, still, they didn't consider going back. They would rather have been torn to pieces by a three-headed dragon waiting for them at the end of the world than die forsaking honor by turning back from their quest. Zulqarnayn had relinquished his will, becoming the tired hero of his own legend. All he had now was a fistful of life. What's more, he hadn't spoken with Hızır in a long while. If he were to speak, clots of black blood would pour from his mouth. Even though Hızır rode right beside him, upon his grey horse, when they fought back to back against their enemies, all Zulqarnayn felt of his milk brother was the warmth of his spine.

There was a river in the distance, barely discernible through the fog. They could tell from its sound that it surged with the strong gravitational pull of the spring equinox. It was the sound of a creature condemned to the proclivities of sun and moon, a creature turning only toward its home. Since time immemorial, rivers like this have never had a fixed abode. Either they can't confine their flow to the channels they've forged, or the day comes when these channels no longer suit them. As Zulqarnayn's army

approached the river, the purple crowns of the man-
drakes appeared along the periphery. They led their
tottering horses by their halters, passing a colossal tree
as tall as thirty men. The tree's cupped leaves were still
water-green, its stone-colored trunk cracked all over.
It was an old tree of worship, a scion of the human
race. They were all overcome with an acute feeling of
helplessness, and they grimaced hungrily, as if their
stomachs had begun to ache as one. Left to their own
instincts, the horses slept on their feet, dreaming of
the miraculous water they sought.

The river was the color of mud, and from overhead
it resembled a gold chain. Afraid of sinking into the
loam that sluiced down off the high cliffsides, the men
stood as far away as possible to behold this imposing
being, this monster whose exquisite rage devoured
their civilizations. There were neither settlements nor
any trace of humans nearby. It was as if everything had
been submerged in water. While some of the soldiers
carved their names into the stones, a habit cultivated
in the zeal of their conquests, Zulqarnayn beckoned
his cook and requested a dried mackerel. It seemed
as though hope had brought Zulqarnayn back to life.
Blood flowed back into his face. He leapt upon the
stones with the eagerness of a young man, making his
way toward the shallowest part of the river. His cook

followed closely behind, tremulous and loyal, keeping his eyes on the mossy stones beneath his feet. First, Zulqarnayn looked into the water, an exaggerated grandeur about his movements. He took the mackerel in one hand and held it in the air, as if casting a spell. This was the latest in a long line of fish that Zulqarnayn had let loose in springs, in ponds, in frog-filled creeks, even in puddles of fetid water, all building up to his arrival here, at the River of Gold. But the fish sank to the bottom of its bed. When Zulqarnayn turned around, he felt more defeated than ever, unable to stomach the incontrovertible lifelessness of the fish. The pain in his side rose to his cheeks, and his eyes began to water.

There were forty dried mackerel left in the cook's satchel. Zulqarnayn gave one to Hızır and distributed the rest to his soldiers, sharing his defeat with them one by one. He must have truly, finally understood that he was not worthy of everlasting life. Yet he seemed resolved. "Whoever can bring the fish to life," he said to them, "that person is the true Zulqarnayn." And so, filled with Zulqarnayn's melancholy, each of them led his tired horse toward the place that he believed was the source of the River of Gold.

—

Suppose that you and I have been hungry for seven days. We've eaten unripe blackberries, left each other a couple morsels of meat from the birds we've hunted. We go mad night after night, itching, nettled by sinister grasses. We pass through thick fogs, soaking ourselves to the bone. We haven't once thought to eat our share of the dried mackerel, still hoping that we might be the real Zulqarnayn, the one who might attain immortality. The air there is cooler. The rainclouds form a thick sheath, letting no light through the vaulted sky. Our eyes are wide, our pupils dilated. The only sounds are the fluttering of wings and the babbling of water. The silence listens to itself alone. Far below, the river licks the earth with an implacable sound. We stand in a marshy clearing, the jade stones on the ground splintering light into the air. An abundance of wellsprings lie before us, eroding the stones from which they trickle forth. The soldiers scatter in all directions, carrying their mackerel. The horses are restless. Zulqarnayn looks down at the river from a steep rock, so close to falling, his back turned on what's about to happen.

Hızır embarks toward one of the most remote springs. He walks slowly, cunningly, as if he knows he won't return. The spring he's chosen is quite puny; it smells bitterly of mold, its water dribbling off the rocks in a thin rivulet that collects in a wide hollow below. Since the water in the hollow converges with a cloudy, widening stream farther along, he thinks, this must be the place where the River of Gold begins. At first, Hızır hesitates as to whether he should cast the mackerel in the water. Perhaps he's thinking about death's chastening power, or worse, its strangling unease. Perhaps he ruminates on how no single son of man deserves immortality, especially given the moral burden of the immeasurable blood spilled during Zulqarnayn's quest; how, even for one who did deserve it, immortality would also be a kind of punishment; how eternal life would be so exhausting, would feel impossible to bear at times; how in fact that elixir of life would thus be a poison, a curse. But then the lust for immortality takes over, and Hızır finds himself taking the dried fish by the tail and slowly lowering it into the water. Phosphorescent irises flash up in the fish's eyelids. Hızır's heart turns to stone. He has lost his humanity. He lifts the half-alive mackerel out of the water and looks probingly into its eyes, feeling deep within himself his own translation to a different realm; like a snake shedding its skin he has been swiftly stripped of desire and longing, of feelings of envy and vengeance from which he had always sought salvation. No one would ever again be warmed by his breath. This is probably the last thing he feels, the ceaseless unease of being forever suspended in the realm of the intermediate, of being between mortal and angel. He takes no time to question which reality ushered forth this miraculous moment, this moment that upended the laws of nature, because something compels him into the water. It is glacially cold, and Hızır shivers from head to toe, for the last time. Swimming after the reanimated fish, he does not marvel at the will to live that propels a fish or bird from its egg, but thinks instead of a young woman on the shore of another river, of the strange pleasure she feels at causing death with her own hands.

Or perhaps you've always wanted a Hızır, one who would prove to you this story is true.

The year you turned twenty-five, you went to your grandmother's village in Dersim to collect the deed to the walnut grove you inherited from her. You found yourself not in the fabled village of her endless stories, but in a place broken off from the world, a place where hardly anything stirred except the black smoke pluming from the chimneys. This village, hidden away like remorse, cut off by the mountains, forgotten there along with its gods. You realized as soon as you got off the minibus that you didn't belong to this orphaned homeland; this homeland where the gendarmerie roam freely with their Kalashnikovs, where the Americans hunt shamelessly for gold in the mines on the far side of the mountains. The gendarmerie kept stopping you on your way to the village, checking your ID each time, asking the same questions: *why do you have a camera, are you a journalist, who are you visiting, why are you here.* Their rage was so meaningless it irritated you. They smelled of motor oil and iron, and you felt stupid when you explained that you enjoy taking photographs. Quite aside from the feeling of anxiety induced by the enormous carvings of commando figures upon the stones, the whole place was shrouded in a kind of glacial ether. All the missing—the people buried under avalanches, the families murdered after the rebellions of '38, those who chased after strange sounds and never returned—seemed to wander as ghosts, their sorrow unremittingly alive. You were scared to death that the mountains that rose up around the village might begin to speak, might tell you that you had gotten off the minibus at the wrong stop. Your fleece-lined boots looked ridiculous on your feet, making crunching noises as you walked through the snow. You were a tourist who had lost her way.

The dogs were the first to welcome you to the village, circling you, sniffing at your heels. One by one, the villagers began to gather around you, as if they'd been informed about your arrival ahead of time. They spoke half in Turkish, half in Zaza, so you couldn't quite understand their words. But you realized as soon as you looked at their faces why your grandmother didn't, couldn't, talk about those tragic events. You understood why, at each attempt, she would break off with a faint cry before she'd even begun. Shame hung like a veil between you and the villagers. Their faces, furrowed from the rays of light glinting off the snow, also bore other lines, etched deep by sharp memories. A caustic knowledge had settled into those lines. Nobody among them had the strength to tally up everything that had happened in this place. They were still scared. Mostly, though, they were curious about you: *who are you, who is your family, why did you come to the ends of the earth in this bleak midwinter?* And though you tried to tell them about the walnut grove left behind by your grandmother, the words piled up in your mouth, like bits of food you could neither swallow nor spit out.

You seemed so chimeric that at first, they were afraid you might be Zurrek. Zurrek, which means something like "fib," is the name of a malicious spirit who takes human form to cause trouble during meals. There are seven hungry pixies hidden inside Zurrek's chest, so when she sits down to eat, she is insatiable. She devours everything inside her host's home in order to feed her pixies. On the first night, they decided that you would sleep in Huriye's home. Huriye had been widowed at a young age and spent most of her time contemplating the veil that divided this world from the other. This was how they tried to ascertain whether you were an unexpected guest or an evil spirit. You were so timid as you sat on the floor to eat with her. You didn't know where to put your feet, and you tried to avoid her sharp eyes staring at you as you blew on your soup.

Huriye kept saying this word you didn't recognize,

pisimlay, before breaking bread, before adding coal to the stove, before any task. It was only much later that you realized this word, this unceasing mantra on everyone's tongue, was "Bismillah": in the name of God. "Pisimlay" was a way of preempting misfortune. It made the fire burn, the yogurt ferment, the sun rise, the Munzur River flow. If something bad happened to someone—if someone's horse got sick, for instance, or if a child fell and scraped her knee, or if someone hadn't received a letter for seven weeks from her fiancé who was away on military service—it was because that person must have done something without a "pisimlay." The reason for Huriye's conspicuously imperious, self-confident manner was those "pisimlays" racing out of her mouth in a sharp whisper. Beginning everything with this enchanted word, she touched the world with the hand of God in everything she did.

Thanks to Huriye's support, it didn't take long for the villagers to be convinced that you weren't an evil spirit, and they began to shower you with their hospitality. You stayed in a new home every night, and each new threshold you passed over added to your sacred aura. The walls of these low-pitched village homes were plastered not with thought but with densely tempered feelings. You got lost there, amid the spirits that hung in midair, amid the fables, amid the stories of what had happened.

On the fourth day after your arrival, while staying in the home of the newlyweds Sırma and Zülfü, you awoke to a strange noise. It sounded as if a group of people were descending through the village, moving in a strangely intense procession; the crowd contained a multitude of voices, voices that sometimes laughed in playful jubilation, and sometimes let out pained groans. You leapt out of bed and looked out the window. You couldn't see anything in that white night, illuminated only by the blanket of snow. Then a hand gently touched your shoulder. You screamed out in fear. Sırma shushed you, her greengage-colored eyes wide.

"Don't you dare look out the window," she said.

Your legs were numb.

"Those sounds," you asked, "where are they coming from?"

Sırma told you, as if she was explaining something completely ordinary, that it was the middle of the month of Hızır, so all the djinns and spirits were traveling to Snake Mountain together in order to commemorate him. If they spot you in the middle of the night, they take you far up into the mountains and you're never seen again. Your mouth hung open in astonishment. Sırma paused, then tucked you back in and looked intently into your eyes; I think she must have realized you weren't convinced. Before she turned off the light, she told you that undue curiosity would bring bad luck, that you mustn't ask anyone questions whose answers you couldn't understand.

When you awoke the following morning, you thought at first that you had had a nightmare. Here in this superstitious climate, your subconscious must have been reliving one of those fables you had heard from the villagers. In your dream, Sırma had seemed much taller than she really was, her hair falling to her waist, strange beads hanging from the strands. When she cautioned you again over breakfast, warning you never to look out the window at night, no matter what—and never to even think of going outside, since crossing the threshold might disturb a spirit who had set her table out front—you thought that the sounds you'd heard in the night might have belonged to some memory that was moving through space, the inner voice of the village's history. You thought you had witnessed a memory belonging to a group of people who had once made their way toward Snake Mountain; it was a memory that swung in the pendulum of timelessness. A couple of hours after Sırma's repeated admonitions, you came to the conclusion that you had merely let the lore delude you. As such, even though these superstitions indulged your aesthetic sensibilities, you refused to allow them to conquer your mind. And you certainly wouldn't condone letting the djinn get the better of you. Still, you didn't get out of bed at night for the rest of your time there. You stopped drinking water as night approached, and if, in spite of all your precautions, you still had to pee, you would simply clench your legs and ignore the impulse. Eventually, though, you came to accept that here, the experience of night was not for humans. During the day, people would go about their business at dizzying speeds, their "pisimlays" resounding in the air; but as the sky darkened, they would grow timid, tiptoeing across their pathways as softly as possible while they took care of the rest of their errands. Night was a forbidden kingdom to them. When everyone climbed into bed and fell asleep, other beings came to life in their homes, where the walls were decorated with pictures of Ali and his sword Zulfiqar. The following morning, they would stand before the sun, which they saw as God's greatest glory, and thank Him for allowing them to survive another night; they would press their lips to the cornerstones glowing in the first light of dawn; it was their way of kissing the sun directly. But you who felt such joy in staying up at night, you and your obsession with the moon and stars, you were an ill-mannered spirit wandering among them.

—

There was a very old Alevi man in the village whose silvery beard reached down to his chest. Frik Dede was a tired, cranky, humpbacked man whose spirit dragged along the ground behind him. It was hard not to try and assign some meaning to his solitude; but more conspicuous than his inscrutability was his worldlessness. He had a world, to be sure, but it was in another place entirely. He was fated to a world where language had dried up, where he could look only inward, where his heart beat so faintly that not even he could hear it. Whatever he looked at with his hollow eyes would suddenly become impossibly distant. He hardly paid you any heed, apart from an occasional timid wave. He wouldn't talk to anyone, but when he plucked the strings of his saz, his melodies broke the heart. Every day at sunset he hobbled to the Munzur River. On nights when he made this journey in a snowstorm, it was as if the cold couldn't ply his flesh, the only sign of its impact the frost in his beard. At first, you thought Frik Dede was mute, but it turned out he'd sworn himself to silence. Ever since his son had been burned alive by a military captain during the military coup, he shut himself up, never opening his mouth again, refusing to form a single sentence except to ask his wife for water. Apart from letting out a deep moan every so often, not a single syllable escaped his lips.

One night, you decided to follow Frik Dede all the way to the Munzur. Though he knew he was being followed, he didn't turn back once during the hour-long journey. And though your ears ached from the cold, he persevered with tremendous resilience in his rubber shoes and a tattered sweater, undaunted by the snowflakes whipping against his face. As he reached the bank of the river, he kneeled down and watched the water for a long time. He began to sway back and forth and speak to the Munzur. You couldn't quite figure out whether he was conversing or praying. He took a piece of bread out of his pocket and placed it on the rock beside him, then set a candle on another rock already covered in molten wax. It was clear that this was a private place of communion for him. The relationship he had with the river suggested the existence of another being, ethereal as the flame on the candle but corporeal enough to consume his offering of bread. There at the riverside, you were at the threshold of some hidden life, one you could neither approach nor turn away from, one that exceeded the limits of your consciousness. Stuck between the august mountains and that river that defied the sky with its murmuring, you were a phantom, trembling in place.

In Dersim, sometimes people vanish into the ether. As you looked at the Munzur, you were looking at the source of the human capacity to become nothing. The connection between Frik Dede and Munzur exceeded the one between you and me; they were tied together by a thread of light. The river became a man, the man a river, and they spoke and listened to each other in a language without alphabet, without form. Frik Dede's bony hands, outstretched toward the river, caressed every face in the world, but you, you were deprived of that caress, and you trembled from head to toe. When you eventually learned the legend of Munzur, you realized that this unsettling scene was merely the latest encounter of a longstanding intimacy, and you sensed ever so slightly that many of its people, people whose joys had gone up in the same flames as their sorrows, looked upon the Munzur to feel the water's glimmering presence.

Once upon a time, there was a shepherd named Munzur. Centuries after the families of the Sayyids had intermingled with the shamans and settled in Dersim, and centuries before the people of Dersim survived the massacre of '38 and scattered to the four corners of the country; in an age when paganism and Alevism bled together like ebru paints, when the Sufi mystic saints and the great tribes had not yet differentiated; when the mountains beyond the sultan's care were classified as the Ottomans' Kurdish Frontier and quickly forgotten; when sages and their disciples established dervish lodges, when bards wrote ballads in the free words of the Kurdish language and sang their hearts out for their beloveds: Munzur was a young man who roamed the mountainsides and plateaus in solitude. In those times, every village had a dervish lodge where the holy wailed in unison; every lodge had at its head a sheikh with a skirt worth kissing; every sheikh had a miracle he'd performed; and every miracle had a witness to spread its glory from tongue to tongue. Munzur, the servant of a saintly agha in a village of Ovacık, lived outside the turmoil of all this consecration, and was by all accounts a rather meek person. He would avert his gaze whenever he appeared before his agha, and avoided everyone with an incivility he'd learned from the mountains. Nobody ever noticed him at crowded banquets or weddings, he was so aloof. To his plow-pulling bulls and his load-bearing colts, though, he was like a tender father; he grazed his sheep on the cliffs where the finest thyme thrived; and for the sheepdog who never left his side, he scattered soft straw in a hollow of the earth so that it could sleep comfortably. Every animal, from snake to centipede, from raven to dove—even the swarms of bees that surged from the beehives—howled, buzzed, chirped, and bleated to express their ease with Munzur. Yet he was ignorant of the intimacy conveyed by these wild noises, unable to realize his innate capacity to converse with the spider as it spun its web. Not only did Munzur disavow the notion of his own self-worth, he considered his transient existence on this earth akin to a dry leaf falling from its branch.

In the autumn of one particularly bountiful year when the rains were plenty, the granaries full of wheat at harvest time, and the ewes birthed twice the usual number of lambs, Munzur's agha decided to go on a distant journey. His intention was to pass through Karbala to pay tribute to the sons of Imam Ali, to make a sacrifice for the poor there to thank

God for his own wealth, and then continue on his pilgrimage to Mecca. So he entrusted everything to Munzur—hearth and home, goods and chattel, wife and children—and bade farewell to his wife in case he never returned.

Nothing changed in Munzur's life in the agha's absence. Just as he always had, he gathered his flock midmorning and disappeared from sight, to return near sundown. Munzur was unaware of the emptiness the agha left behind; and similarly, the agha never thought of Munzur on the road, even once, as he was to purge his preoccupied mind of the tedium of worldly affairs. As chance would have it, though, the agha was afflicted with an unexpected illness on his journey. One night while sojourning at an inn in Syria, he began to tremble uncontrollably. He trembled with such violence that no matter how many quilts, animal hides, and goat hair blankets the innkeeper piled upon him, he wouldn't warm up. The agha struggled helplessly to fend off the penetrating cold, curled up and purple underneath the heap of covers. The whites of his eyes were leaden, and the more he shivered, the more his belly swelled and his kidneys ached. For some reason, the agha, undaunted his whole life by so many snowstorms, by avalanches that swallowed people up at a moment's notice, by crop-sullying frosts, couldn't ascertain the source of that trembling inside him. Meanwhile, the agha's wife had been praying night and day for her husband to return safe and sound. Late that very night, she was frying helva. Whether because she craved it or because she wanted to accustom herself to the idea of her husband's death, who knows. But as the kitchen filled with its funerary vapors, she was seized by the panic of having to spend the rest of her life watching and waiting for her husband. There is nothing worse, after all, than watching and waiting. The wife of the agha knew that those who go missing, those who leave and do not return, cause more pain than the dead. Rather than subject herself to his indefinite absence, she resigned herself to the fact of her husband's death and continued cooking the helva. After doling it out to all the neighbors, she brought a plate to Munzur.

"Oh," she sighed before he took a bite, "I wish your agha was here to taste this helva."

"Don't worry, mistress," Munzur replied, "I'll bring it to him." And he left the room.

No sooner had Munzur taken a step out into the pitch-dark night than he found himself inside a large room with stone walls girded by wooden beams, surrounded by hanging oil lanterns. The agha was curled up in bed, shaking, drenched in cold sweat. As soon as he saw Munzur there, carrying a plate of steaming helva, his ashen pallor grew suddenly darker. It seemed to him that Azrael had decided to appear before him in the image of the most innocent person he'd ever known. The agha must have been one of God's anointed servants, though, for he would be able to taste the helva made for his funeral before he had even drawn his final breath; to have the last morsel that passed one's lips be made by someone he loved, it was a privilege bestowed on very few men. Just before he pronounced the shahadah and embraced his death, he noticed that the eyes of the man who stood before him were not the soulless eyes of an angel; it really was his Munzur. Munzur held the plate of helva out with his usual diffidence, saying in a soft voice, "Here, my agha." The agha started from bed in fear, his cheeks ruddy. He took the dish, scooped up the helva, and returned the empty plate to Munzur. In the time it took the agha to blink, Munzur had vanished.

Nobody, least of all Munzur himself, would have thought him capable of performing such a miracle. As soon as he returned home, still carrying the empty plate, he kneeled down and beseeched God to assure him that what had just transpired wasn't real. Let's say, he told himself, that I ate the helva myself, and fed it to my agha in a dream.

Three years later, on a spring day when the clouds had descended to the earth, a man with a beard down to his belly appeared in the distance on the back of a sorrel horse. He was a pitiful man; his shoulders withered, his coat in rags and tatters. Nobody recognized him until he arrived in the village square. Only when the agha's wife embraced the wretch and kissed his hands did they realize who he was. Children, men, and women, everyone flocked around him excitedly. But the agha's eyes searched for Munzur, who stood on the fringes of the crowd; God willing, the agha wouldn't see him there. Munzur wished, impossibly, that the offering of helva might have been forgotten; he didn't want it to be flung in his face. But his wish didn't come true. While everyone in the crowd jostled to kiss the agha's hands, the agha pushed through the crowd looking for his tender Munzur. As soon as he saw him, standing with his head bowed like a ripe ear of wheat, the agha held his arms out toward him.

"That shepherd is the one whose hands you should be kissing. I have witnessed his miracles, I can attest to them."

Munzur simply couldn't bear being put on display like this. When everyone turned to look at him, they saw in his place a divine being disguised as a shepherd. Not knowing what to do, Munzur took two steps backward. Never in his entire life had he wanted someone to attest to his virtue, nor had he ever wanted his existence to be so conspicuous. When the villagers approached him, their bearing speaking their reverence, Munzur turned and ran for his life. Those who saw him sprinting toward the mountains claimed that water sprung from the earth he tread upon, that the white-foamed river that cleansed Dersim from top to bottom had opened up along the path he ran. Perhaps there had always been a river there, but it had no name until Munzur disappeared, never to return…

—

Frik Dede now stood in that same place, so many thousands of years after Munzur's disappearance. It didn't occur to you, as you watched him, that he might have been communing with the shepherd in whose likeness that river had sprung into being. You thought he was just a father in pain, constricted by silence, speaking to his heart there on the banks of the babbling river. And you were right. This thing called legend isn't just the backbone of narrative keeping this community's spirit alive; it was Frik Dede's only solace in this infernal world, an inner shrine that allowed him to turn his back on the inhumanity of everything else. But looking at the river, you didn't know how to see anything beyond it. Instead of seeing the river for what it truly was and sticking your hand in its icy waters, feeling the cold rise from your numb fingers to the bones of your wrist, you fixed your eyes on Frik Dede, trying to understand what he was doing. And what could I do? I plunged myself into the water when I got bored standing there beside you. Breathing in the water, there among the carp, circumambulating the algae-covered stones without you, I wondered what might compel miracles to stay hidden. When I finally emerged from the river, soaking wet, I'd been cleansed. But you'd turned and gone, dragging your feet and hanging your head. I called after you, I called and I called, but you didn't hear me.

At that moment, I suppose, you must have been thinking about your grandmother again. Over the course of your days in the village, as you grew accustomed to Huriye's irritability, and Sırma's mercurial gaze, and Frik Dede's labored brooding, you couldn't stop yourself from reminiscing about her. So much time had passed since her death, but still, you nourished her melancholy like a tumor in your chest. As you returned from the river to the village, the mystery surrounding her anguish began to fall away, and an image of her came into focus before you. A plaintive moment, a photographic memory, that couldn't be struck from your mind…

It's a winter night in Samsun; because of the dreary

weather, the streets are buried under the smoke of
coal stoves. The buses are jam-packed. Women shout
at the top of their lungs, calling their children home.
You're barely ten years old, sitting on the garden
wall of a house at the top of a cobble-stoned slope,
swinging your legs as you watch the passersby. Your
grandmother slowly emerges into view at the bottom
of the hill. She wears a forest-green overcoat and her
arms are extended, carrying bags from the market.
Her headscarf has slipped off a little. She greets people with a nod as they walk by and lowers her eyes to
the ground; she clearly doesn't want to talk with any
of them. There's a birdlike disquiet in the way she
moves. From afar, her gait is awkward; her neck is
tense, wedged between her straining shoulders. She
pays no heed to the timescape she passes through;
head bent low, she is living in a time of her own.
To her, the world looks desolate, like she has nobody
left to talk to. No matter where she looks, she can't
find herself. But the moment she notices you there, a
broad smile spreads across her face. She smiles not just
with her mouth, but with her nose, her forehead, her
burdened shoulders, smiles with an ardor that suffuses
the whole neighborhood. Like she's seeing a beautiful country. Devotion gleams in her eyes. When that
flawless moment finally ends, a wound opens up in

you, one that will never heal. Even now, it still hasn't dawned on you: no matter where you go, camera in hand, you'll never be able to capture her smile.

Caves make us so primal. Primal not just in mind but in body, too. Sleeping in a cave is like sleeping the sleep of a beast. Your senses become sharper. You begin to hear everything, to discern the layers in every smell; when the snow's surface cracks at the entrance to the cave, you jump to your feet with bestial agility.

The day that you and Zülfü explored the rocky outcroppings on the outskirts of the village, the two of you descended into a cave, undaunted by the icicles, and were immediately struck by the smell of rot. The surfaces of the cave were covered with the last remnants of the present tense: walls etched with names, stones steeped in human breath, putrid shreds of blankets, cigarette butts, crushed beer cans. You sat quietly with Zülfü for a long time. Your ears and the bridge of your nose ached in the unbearable cold. Every time you exhaled, white smoke plumed from your mouth. Zülfü smoked several cigarettes one after the other. His Turkish sometimes slipped into Zaza; he got lost in it before resurfacing for you.

"If not for the bridge," he said, "If not for the Harput Bridge over the Munzur, Dersim would have been hell."

It was thanks to the bridge that many people were

able to flee, and had been saved from the carnage.
Though Zülfü hadn't lived through any of the stories he told, as a child born in Dersim who grew up
amid its deathly wailing and hoarse grumbling, he
told the story of the '38 massacre as if he'd seen it
with his own eyes, stopping and starting the story not
in the secondhand past tense, but in a personal past
tense of his own remembering. He became more than
one of the victims all at once, careful not to omit the
sighs of some old woman or man, speaking with a
voice much older than he was, as if to rebel against
the silence imposed by your grandmother Bese and
by Frik Dede. He was not simply relating the stories
as he had heard them; he was outright remembering
them. Mind you, he was not an individual subject
remembering. His remembrance was expansive,
without center, without bone; it exceeded the locus
of a single pair of eyes, a single body, one's individual
senses. As Zülfü looked upon the past, there from that
cave, looked with the eye of a god who encompassed
all the mountains and caves in Dersim, all the twists
and turns in the Munzur River, all the walnut groves
and forests, with the eye, that is, of a familiar god, one
who can suffer, who can feel agony, it was Hızır you
saw there before you.

And so, the more Zülfü spoke, the more horrible

he became. He told of the unspeakable things that one human can do to another, mincing no words as he carved out of time itself the rawest, most vulgar portrait of tragedy. And like a war photographer can stop her own heart to take heartrending shots that etch themselves into memory, Zülfü too was carving a hole in your heart with his heartless words. He told you, for instance, about a family that took refuge behind their wool mattresses, about how those mattresses were raked by the fire of a Gatling gun, using his hands to illustrate the bloody shreds of wool as they flew through the air. He closed his eyes as he described a baby struggling to nurse at the breast of its dead mother. Zülfü's voice cracked when he told you how they stabbed the baby and threw it into the river so it wouldn't die of hunger. By this point, he had burdened himself with the sin of speaking such cruelties into being; a vague disgust spread across his face from touching upon the sick pleasure that dwells at the core of violence. He deepened your anguish when he told how there were so many corpses thrown into the Munzur that the water was no longer drinkable, and how people had to burn willow branches instead to drink the sap that oozed out; how a mother had to suffocate her fear-stricken son so that his cries wouldn't betray their location to the soldiers, and how she threw herself off the cliffs three days later; how, from far away, the piles of corpses resembled stacks of burlap sacks.

But it was when you heard that an entire family lay buried in the very cave you were in that you felt as though you were literally stepping on the bodies of the dead. Zülfü pointed out the significance of every step you took.

Once upon a time, a young man named Celal lived in Dersim. He was a jealous man by nature, and never let his wife or three children out of his sight. The events leading up to the massacre, which began with the state kidnapping small children, erupted with a soldier raping a woman, and reached fever pitch with the execution of the rebel leaders and the public display of their bodies in the streets of Elazığ; everything spiraled completely out of control after many families were executed en masse by firing squads. When the bombs began to fall from war planes, people hid their valuables in the paunches of dead animals and made to flee across the Harput Bridge. Celal and his wife fled to this cave, carrying their three children on their shoulders and waists. After approximately four days of waiting in fear, they saw the soldiers approaching. Celal drew his prized blade and slit the throats of his children, starting with the youngest. Before he killed his wife, he cried out. "Don't look," he said. "Don't look at me."

As soon as you heard this story you wanted to get out as quickly as possible. It wasn't anguish that you felt, but fear, fear for your life. Rather than offering some kind of redemption, Zülfü's account was alive with the strong possibility that '38 could happen again. The more Zülfü's living tongue spoke the past tense into narrative, the more you became someone who could be killed at any moment.

Defiance flourishes in the shadow of tyranny. Every hero seems to emerge from a nesting doll of tyrants. The splendid words memorialized in city squares, the sermons about freedom, the lines of poetry, they all call to mind the spirits of tyrants unfurling like clouds over a city. All those tablets that extol heroism also teach the methods of evil. The story of Celal, for instance, murdering his family so as not to submit to the enemy, might appear to some as a source of pride. But that leaves you entirely alone with your compassion for his wife, seeing her eyes widen with horror.

Do you remember when you visited the ruins of Xanthos? It was one of those familiar antique cities in Anatolia, of which you'd seen dozens: a city the Lycians, the Persians, the Greeks, and the Romans had passed through over the course of history, razing what they found to the ground before stacking stone upon stone of their own. But you were especially insistent on seeing Xanthos, trekking from Fethiye to Kaş in thirty-five-degree heat. More than the wind-softened stones, what drew you to that lost city was its grisly history. The seductions of violence always lead you down the bends of dusty backroads. You bought your entry ticket from the Ministry of

Culture's office, which consisted of a plastic booth placed at the city's helm; this antique city, where today shepherds graze their sheep on thyme shooting from beneath millennia-old marble tombs. You had no interest in looking at the cracked mosaics, in piecing them back together in your mind. It didn't take very long before you asked the shepherd who was guiding you, helping you visualize the markets in the forum, the priestesses entering and exiting the temples, to point out the location of the agora. The air smelled of sheep dung, but it was blood that made your nostrils flare.

The Persian General Harpagos had come from Asia Minor to conquer the entire region, and after capturing the Greek cities one by one, he arrived on the plains of Xanthos and stood before the Lycians like Azrael. The Xanthian soldiers battled ardently against Harpagos's powerful army, until eventually they had no choice but to retreat. When they understood that Xanthos had been surrounded, that it was about to fall, the soldiers assembled their families in the agora; they burned the people of the city alive, weeping as they did so, leaving not a soul standing before they mounted a suicidal assault on Harpagos. This chilling ceremony of death was what created the legend of Xanthos, what drew you into its midst; this final assertion of will in which soldiers opted to sacrifice themselves instead of being sacrificed.

—

Xanthos passed into the annals of history as the home of this kind of solemn reprisal, and the fact that not a single Lycian survived means that it is remembered for this act of total self-destruction. Yet for some reason, this story is always characterized as an illustration of the repercussions of excessive pride. As if there were two kinds of blood that could be spilled, one representing the righteous violence of the Lycians; the other, Harpagos's wicked violence. Other peoples who later settled in the city were so affected by the history of the Xanthians' obliteration that this fearsome and violent tale became sacred, worthy of their unceasing devotion. When Brutus the Roman occupied the city, six hundred years after that first massacre, the Xanthians reenacted the legend. The fear that they would be killed unless they first killed themselves had come back to haunt them, a memory still fresh so many centuries after the fact. The notion of preventive suicide was carved into their minds. It was an irresistible fate, the only one left to them.

As you left the ruins of Xanthos, a lump lodged in your throat, the shepherd showed you a tree with full, ferocious branches. A deranged olive tree, its bark and leaves a hazy, lusterless green. The shepherd told you that a bottle containing three olive seeds had been uncovered during archaeological excavations four years earlier. The "foreign" archaeologist who found the seeds sent one to Israel and another to his homeland; the third was planted at the entrance to the city of Xanthos, and from it had sprung the shrub that stood before you. As you circled this nearly two-thousand-year-old tree, you felt something open up inside you. That rueful little olive, which had seen the Xanthian soldiers kill their own families, had been able to stitch together a life, all on its own.

It's a tree, after all. Trees always acts differently from humans.

It can't forget,
nor can it
remember.

WAIL

How radiant Istanbul was yesterday! All its edges began to blur, awash in untarnished colors and pure light. As you made your way by taxi to the square in Beşiktaş where the Hıdrellez celebration was taking place, I spent a long time watching a yellow cloud of pollen floating in the air above the city's parks. The pollen drifted toward the Bosphorus, a great consummation taking place overhead, and the atmosphere smelled of flesh. I simply adore that pungent smell, all the seeds of the earth making the world sweat, drop by drop, in their fervor. Every breath of yours delivered the scent of the world to me. There were eyes wide open in the shadows of the plane trees at Dolmabahçe Palace, intent on the flood of people pouring down the street. The trees really did have eyes, and watched with them. But you, you held off on all you could've seen, choosing instead to stare blankly at the crowd flowing down the sidewalk, your camera in your lap. I get so frustrated when you lose yourself in thoughts that obscure my translucent body. I don't know what I can do to show you what I've seen. Your head leaned against the window, bent toward the mortal dark; the mark of an ancient glyph was seared upon your forehead. Ever since you named the fig tree in your garden Zevraki, you've been marked by a deep, omega-shaped sorrow; neither word nor fantasy written on your face. You were a fig that did not exist. Within that absence of time, you nestled at the foot of the tree and spread out on the ground like a patch of shade; you took refuge in the darkness and lost yourself, found yourself again; you were at the very core of a fruit that would never exist, the incarnation of a nothingness that hopes to exist again. I'm curious, have you ever felt Zevraki scrutinizing you? Instead of coveting the dolor of that tree that can't bear fruit, a tree that imbibes its own nectar, why don't you let it see you, why don't you feel the way it looks at you?

Your susceptibility to illusion, your continuous deferral of the present, pleases me sometimes. In fact, your slowness has made you mature faster. Sometimes, as you stare at a shoot growing from the tree, you feel existence surge deep down, ineffably, in your bones. Yet the moment you feel it, you relinquish your own state of being, appearing and disappearing like the flash of a camera's light... For a moment, you are ablaze, then you leave behind your smoky traces. I am always forgotten in your afterimage. Ah, but your unyielding willfulness, the walls you put up that can't be torn down; that's what I resent the most. If only you could savor the absurdity of life. If only you could realize that brooding over Zevraki, coveting its unripe fruits, the remorse with which its branches bear them, is merely a diversion. Then you could hold me close to your breast.

I don't know if you realize it, but you were nothing more than an exile during your time in Dersim. You were a tiny fruit that had fallen to the ground and rolled away. You were the scion of a generation expelled from its lands, a missing generation that had languished in unfamiliar cities and climates, and you consoled yourself with those three dönüms of walnut grove you inherited. That's why the villagers embraced you. That's why their children climbed into your cold bed and blew on your blankets to warm them up. Their many kindnesses frustrated you to no end. After all, you didn't know how to look the mountains in the eyes; you couldn't speak to the sun; you couldn't perceive the wisdom borne by the moonlight. In this place where nature dominated life and defied human will—this place with an unfinished and bloody history, this place where meaning had been blown apart—you watched its people lead their pure lives, trying to make their worlds make sense. It intensified the emptiness inside you. You stood in the center of a world of arcane symbols that operated according to their own self-proclaimed logic. Even the shadows cast by the spiny, bare branches of the walnut trees formed a web of meanings of their own.

But Dersim indulged your lack of understanding, your naïveté. You couldn't quite manage to photograph the feeble light, the dimness, the fire swelling in the hearth, the raw glow of the light bulbs pitching shadows on the walls, the snow that glimmered in spite of the night's darkness. You didn't have a story to tell. Nor could you think of anything to say to them, so you just sat each of them down facing the sun and took their portraits. Sırma, Frik Dede, and Huriye gave forced, melancholy smiles as they stared into your lens. You saw the same sentence written in each of their eyes. The latent phrases described the world-making potential of their agony and their ecstasy.

This place is the country of the invisible; it is the land where Munzur became nonexistent, the place where Hızır is hidden. You were in the originary abode of Hızır, that immortal being who had lived for thousands of years under so many different names. Perhaps Munzur and Hızır were even the same person. Perhaps Hızır was the undying being who traversed the earth and all its ages, and Munzur was merely who he was as a youth in Dersim. Surrounded by mountains, this valley offered no way out; it was a planet where every stone, every tree, every spring was a temple; it was a planet hallowed by beliefs that confounded imams and clerics, far removed from our world in which religion and morality are perpetually in deadlock. Hızır was a god in this valley, visible in every place at any time. He and his grey horse left footprints in the snow; he entered homes and ate meals that had been prepared especially for him; he shuffled up to people as a friend; he offered the people of Dersim, caught between soldiers and guerrillas, access to the boundless divine.

When the three-day fast for Hızır began, the village lapsed into a solemn silence. Their hunger was one of bereavement. This fast did not just discipline the senses; it beseeched the universe for forgiveness, it chased away evil and tried to hold it at bay. The children were expected to be quiet when they played, and women covered their mouths with their hands as they joked with one another, to keep laughter from escaping and spreading among them. Everyone anxiously awaited Hızır's arrival, leaving their front doors half-open and a fire constantly burning in the hearth. The reason they put so much stock in Hızır's visit was that he brought bounty to every home he entered. After sunset, everyone gathered gravely around the kitchen table and broke their fast with a simple meal of ayran and bread. Nobody ate so much as a morsel of meat, nor did they drink a sip of water.

That night, every girl of marriageable age prayed to Hızır to show her a dream. It was said that whoever appeared in the girls' dreams to give them water would be the man they were supposed to marry. All the married village women had met their husbands in these parched visions. Some husbands had emerged from the Munzur River carrying a cupped handful of water; others had come to their bedsides carrying an actual cup; still others had impishly dumped a bucket of water upon their prospective wife. Every aspect of life in this other world revolved around Hızır, took on the symbols of his mandate. But though you left no stone unturned, you never found a trace of Hızır.

Once, unable to restrain yourself, you asked Huriye what he looked like. "Who does he look like?" she echoed. "Like you, like me, like everyone." You saw then how meaningless your question was. He was a being ordinary as sunlight, plain as the branches on a tree. He was no abstraction, but a distant relative who could appear before you when you least expected it. So when you asked Huriye whether or not she had seen Hızır, she told you curtly that seeing him didn't matter, passing the thread further through the eye of her needle.

On the third day of the fast, everyone in the village showed each other the traces that Hızır had left behind: hoof prints left by his horse in the snow, a half-eaten loaf of bread, still-warm cushions where it seemed someone had sat and rested. You couldn't capture any of these moments. The unbounded and solitary melancholy you nourished in your breast for those ten days fizzled out, replaced instead by a coarse feeling of lack. You found yourself losing what your grandmother Bese had already lost long before. You haven't gone back to Dersim since, and I don't think you ever will. If there is a Hızır out there, ordained for you alone, your best shot at finding him was elsewhere.

It's hard to sleep within you. Sometimes, I dream that you think of me, and when I observe you from my own corner of the world, watching the way you live feels like torture. You make time, while I, nestled here in your rib cage, smoke it; I am a wound, etching itself upon your lungs day by day. I always see you alone in my dreams. When I see you squabble with Zevraki, or peek out at the world through your camera, or lose your composure during heated arguments, or pace unsteadily through your house, your eyes and head hanging toward the ground, I feel in my breast your bitter failure to hold your desires in abeyance. Your feelings brush up against me, become stones, tumble into the darkness. I'm stuck here among those stones. My waist and back ache and ache. You become an insurmountable wall between me and the world. That's why I love celebrations. Your stomach, your heart, your temples, all those places inside you that have grown weary of resisting the world, give up, if only briefly, on their ruminating. The task of entering the crowd falls to me alone.

You always cling so tightly to yourself whenever those around you are enjoying themselves, clasping your hands to your chest in order to slip through the crowd, holding me close to your heart, unwilling to give anything of yourself up to anyone. Your hands are filled with the same sense of security you used to feel when you slept clutching stones. I love it when you're like this, I really do. There is an innocent trepidation about you, a suspicion of strangers, a fear of letting your spirit slip through your fingers. Your ignorance is incandescent. But as you get used to the crowd, your eyes begin to shrink, they tire of worrying. Light doesn't pass through your irises. I don't know if it's because all happy faces look alike, but you begin to regain your composure, comforted by their uniformity. Your cheeks begin to blush. You relish the feeling of being one of them, becoming invisible, disappearing in the eyes of others. The chasm between who you believe yourself to be and who you are in reality begins to close. In such moments, the past that reigns over the present tense suddenly loses its force. These moments when you are unburdened of the past are a gift of the festivities that take place in city squares, in makeshift markets down winding alleyways. Your conscious mind goes pure white, untainted for a moment; your melancholy is nullified. Surrounded by crowds of people, all your senses go numb. When this happens, you spring forth as an eager, gregarious person, alert and full of life. I swing off your sinews without your noticing, and release myself silently down, slipping out of your dreams.

—

When we arrived at Ahırkapı last night I had long since split from you, an immeasurable distance between us. You were the imaginary body then, and I the real. The sidewalk you stood upon, the sky you looked up at when you got out of the taxi, the Byzantine fortress walls just behind you: each was the cornerstone of a fictional setting, part of a plane where I don't exist, but which I possess and can sense, even smell, so intimately. You were the protagonist of my novel, ready to do everything I want her to yet incapable of knowing what the next sentence will hold. You were the figure of a woman not yet defeated, yet you still guarded a paradox, the mystery of which I couldn't resolve. I could see the lump in your throat when you swallowed, but couldn't comprehend the burden of the future that you felt as you held your breath. Despite my authorly audacity, I still worried about you. Right before you slipped into that sweeping emptiness, you stood still for a long time, awash in the evening light, staring at the opposite shore, at all the lights ablaze in people's homes. The songs bellowed by the drunk crowds gathering on the waterfront had soured your expression. You had no inclination to celebrate Hıdrellez.

You acted as though you'd happened upon the celebration by accident, rather than chosen to come there of your own free will. You were a stranger who had entered this world without parents, entirely alone, desolate and drifting. A misfit, without ancestors, without nationality, the chambers of her memory completely vacant. I couldn't take my eyes off of you, afraid that I wouldn't ever be able to enter back inside you. I approached you quickly and smelled your breath; olives. In the warm halo of spring you were so soft, so permeable, that I could return whenever I wished, but there was still something so bland about you, withdrawn as you were. I followed you for a while as you made your way toward the crowd, shrouded under smoke that fumed from the fish grills and tripe carts. You walked indecisively. It was hard to see anything clearly under that aromatic cloud, except for people's heads moving about and their smiles gleaming. It seemed to you that everyone was sharing their bodies with one another. The mirth of those throngs, verging on ecstasy, was singular. With every step your nose burned, your eyes watered, and your neck involuntarily withdrew. Pulling your camera out of its case, you were stoic as a soldier about to aim her weapon at an enemy. I didn't long for you then; I stood back as far as possible, far from your hungry gaze that idealizes faces, from your eye that simplifies even as it exalts. Leaving the waterfront and passing inside the ancient fortress walls, I was struck first by the tang of urine coming from the portable toilets, then the appetizing smells of köfte and beer. Ahırkapı was generally a quiet area, apart from the wedding festivities of the Romani families that lived there, which often lasted until morning; now, though, it was jam-packed with people, including wide-eyed tourists poking around and musicians carrying their instrument cases toward the pubs where they would perform that night. The streets of this Romani neighborhood, stranded between hotels and the big, bay-windowed homes that were operated as hostels, had entirely lost their allure. Ribbons had been tied around everything, even in the narrow alleyways that draw people along meandering routes and into the neighborhood's confidence. Everything from electricity poles to balcony railings, from clotheslines to radio antennae on parked cars, had been knotted with streamers and pieces of fabric, turning the whole place into a brightly colored shrine. This enormous tapestry, to which everyone coming to the festivities had contributed, was the curtain behind a crowded stage

that harbored both the sacred and the profane. Those
who wanted to cast off their misery, to find love, to
reunite with something or someone they'd lost; those
who had begged and pleaded for these things all
year; and those who had grown tired of sacrifice and
consigned themselves to reproach: all were gathered
together at the same time. Nor was I set apart. As I
observed this tabernacle of desire, of which I, too, was
a part, I kept an eye on you as you pushed and shoved
and brushed against other people's body parts in order
to make your way through the crowd. Unavoidable
intimacy. Everyone fell into step with one another
as they danced, face to face, striving to conserve the
warmth that flowed from flesh to flesh in that great
embrace, unbothered by the stinging scent of sweat,
the onioned breath licking their faces.

The music was lively, a karcığar melody. The songs
played by the Romani musicians tugged at our heart-
strings. Filled with the spontaneous desire to hop, to
bounce their shoulders, to swing their heads, nobody
remained still; the crowd began advancing toward the
stage in familiar dance configurations. Amid all this
exuberance, the musicians exuded an air of penury.
Although the red cummerbunds around their waists
endowed them with elegant uniformity, their sullied
cuffs and the worn knees of their black pants divulged

their desolation. Theirs was a veiled poverty. The members of the Ahırkapı orchestra had tamed their wild instruments and, in the spontaneous strength of their unison, had pledged themselves to the most pompous form of positivity. The world truly seemed to be fiction as you listened to them; pain, poverty, separation, grief, none of it was real. The only truth at Ahırkapı was the undulating melody of the karcığar, oscillating between the neva in the key of D and the hicaz in the C. The music coalesced in a sonic narrative, the clarinet creeping into the melancholy warbling of the oboe-like zurna, the thumping of the drum coming in immediately after. With the playful entrance of the strings, the music switched to a çargah, a melody that unexpectedly recalled the way birds of prey take sudden flight while hunting. This particular awe-inspiring sequence was a nikriz, a time-honored chord progression. The gestures of nature, of hawk and eagle, of the decisive moment when an owl dives from its nest in pursuit of a small creature in the field below, all spun through the air, the ineffable world taking form in sound. The dancers stretched their arms out as if to take flight, closing their eyes, losing themselves at last in the playful rhythm of the darbuka drum. I watched them, watched the way they felt in the thumping of their blood the fear of the little creature fleeing in the field, watched them vacillate between the roles of prey and predator. Their dance was a harmony of dread and pleasure, the essence of an ancient ritual consecrating the boundless affinity we feel with every other creature inhabiting this earth. The dancers weren't just making wishes there that night; they were also expressing their gratitude. That's where I finally discovered what you're missing, the rip in the atlas of your spirit plain as day before me: it was gratitude itself, woven into the very lining of existence…

—

After night fell in earnest, the musicians moved on to a more playful song. That's when a young man caught my eye. He was such a good dancer; I couldn't take my eyes off him. It seemed like his feet stepped elsewhere, even though he was right there before me, his arms raised above his head, drawing intricate patterns in the air, caressing the music. The harsh spotlights made him appear flat, like a shadow on a curtain. With great difficulty, I made my way beneath one of the spotlights in order to see him better, and found you right across from me. You stood under the other spotlight, watching him intently. We were the opposite ends of a line that pierced through both our chests. We were two shapes, symmetric, the dancing man traversing the line that strung us together. Your camera hung around your neck, its mechanical eye still shuttered.

The crowd had receded slightly, opening up space for the young man. There was a natural halo about him. You imagined that he had been endowed with it when he was born, that nobody could enter his periphery without his consent. You watched, unblinking, as he strung the music around himself with enviable ease, moving his body in effortless sync with the rhythm. There was a girlish daintiness about him as well. He couldn't really be characterized as manly or womanly. He exuded an air of tenderness, masculine and feminine charm commingling in the same body. Every time he threw his head backward, drops of sweat flew off his wet hair, scattering his bliss generously; he looked into the eyes of his spectators and smiled, as though he'd known each of them a long time. At one point his black leather jacket slipped off his shoulders. Gazing upon his bare collarbone, the throbbing vein in his neck, his Adam's apple, his nape, I felt a fiery trembling in the tangle of wires leading to my groin. His exuberant flesh glimmered before me, tender in contrast to his ash-colored face. An unfaded body kept secret in a chamber of my memory, whose scent I recognized from long ago, whose breathing I have listened to time and again, whose salts I have tasted. This, I think, is desire, when affection for a stranger bursts into bloom.

That's when I looked back at you. Your eyes were open wide, a rapt smile spread across your face. It almost looked like you were going to step toward him, wriggle through the crowd, open your arms wide to dance. But what did you do instead? You rose up resolutely and, nimbly removing the lens cover, raised your camera to your eye as if taking aim. Your face disappeared. One eye closed, the other on the viewfinder, your mouth hanging open, your chest bent forward. You participated in this dance by withdrawing completely into yourself, using that lens to conjure distance between the two of you. Quickly depressing the shutter-release button, trying to capture whatever reality that light brought to bear upon the scene. You were nothing more than a fellow traveler, following the same route. In the instant they struck your camera's complex of articulated mirrors, the frozen images of the dancing man, every pose in which he opened his mouth wide as if to bite into the sky, every shot in which his body, tensed like a bow, appeared in the negative like a pitch-black ghost, was transformed into a farewell proffered by the dead; a gentle murder. With every fatal assault of your index finger, you were not merely content to put an end to the ecstasy of this man who had immersed his entire being in the music, you also lamented time's merciless and inexorable passing. As you deftly sculpted the joy you so envied into sentimental snapshots, the dancing man was unaware of your voyeurism, of your gaze that refuses to accept the world as it appears, of his own transformation into a vulgar symbol, into a symbol of abandon, tasked with filling the emptiness in your mind, exhibited in a manner even he would find strange, exalted by the effects of light and shadow...

I watched you take pictures for a long time, watched you biting your lower lip over and over again out of excitement. You had dedicated yourself to seeking out the ineffable, to capturing the common humanity it shows, and you held your breath every time you pressed the shutter button, petrified, becoming one with your camera. Then you pranced about in pursuit of the dancing man, stooping and standing up amid the crowd, appearing and disappearing and reappearing, climbing onto a pile of vegetable crates, even clambering onto the railings of balconies, brazenly pushing people's heads out of the frame, drawing surreptitious circles around him. Yet somehow his resplendent ineffability eluded you.

Your light settings were incorrect, so all you got were crooked images of him, bent and broken, skewed, either simpering or overly subdued, fuzzy and superimposed, most of them blurry and shaky. I could tell by the way you kept scowling at the camera screen. Perhaps because you focused more out of desire than curiosity, every shot you took betrayed your clumsiness, that you'd never learned to take part in the lives of others, that you didn't know how to erase your contempt from your photographs. No matter what you tried, no matter what you did, you simply couldn't consummate with the world.

"My eye!"

That's what your grandmother called you once as she caressed you, that antiquated term of endearment derived from colloquial language. Had she christened you her third eye so that you might see what she couldn't? If that eye she bestowed is more than just sight, perception, light, and witnessing, if it is in fact her intrinsic inheritance, then you should know that every time you raise your camera and point it like a telescope, zooming in and out on the world, you are carving that eye out of yourself, eviscerating your inheritance. No sooner have you looked at something than you begin to alter it. Every time you take an object into your viewfinder, you tear it from the world, give it a shape of your own devising, as if life is composed merely of those moments you fix in place; you seek what is timeless through your compositions instead of finding it first in people's faces.

What if you called me "my eye," just once, out of love; what if you put my translucent body there on your forehead and we found so many frames together, preserved things without plundering them, finding the eternity in a fraction of a second, without praise or rebuke; what if we nullified all qualities, private and public, polite and vulgar, and confessed there's something we can't see where we look; what if we went quiet, together, without boasting of our prudence: wouldn't that be beautiful? Just say the word, and I'll give up my eye for you.

How still you are now. Sleep suits you. You're on the verge of trickling out of that chair. Head tossed to one side, hair hanging down, thighs interlocked, elbows propped up on the armrests: you've built a roof out of yourself. The afternoon's soft light caresses you in rays blanching the tulle curtains. You are a lithe body, a resplendent shape; your chest expands and contracts, then contracts and expands anew, and I am warmed along with the breath in your lungs. You have not fallen asleep but awakened to a dream. All the peach fuzz on your body stands on end. You peer inside yourself through your pores, which are eyes. Whatever it is you see, you dwell on my words with your life itself.

—

Here you are, entering a grand temple. The vaulted iwan in the front wall is so wide that your first step disturbs your sense of terrestrial space. The inner walls are covered in gold, your reflection stretched out on the blue marble floor. Another even grander room awaits beyond the antechamber, filled with the aroma of pine, and you find yourself enchanted in this atmosphere, lights twinkling off the amber in the fine cedar panels sheathing the walls. The ceiling is adorned with motifs of date palms and fig trees, the corners with reliefs of doves, wings open, about to take flight. Moving deeper into the hall, you reach a massive statue of a falcon, its tail feathers fanned. You lean on the pillar beside you, pomegranate baubles dangling from it like precious earrings. There are others here, too, standing quietly with their heads down.

Look! A king sits across from you, excoriating the crowd from his pearl-encrusted throne. The vein on his forehead is throbbing. In the leopard fur slung across his back is a shibboleth, a tale that nobody knows how to decipher. Some say that it bears the secret of the universe, but is rendered illegible by the fur's black and yellow convolutions. Others claim there's no shibboleth at all, only the king himself, the way the pelt on his back shows what the leopard has and he lacks. If the leopard now lacks its tail, it is only because the king's tale was insufficient itself.

This man is my Solomon, the king who should not have been born, for whom all taboos were broken; King Solomon, whose mother Bathsheba fell in love with David while she was still married to a Hittite officer. Whether because shame and love commingled in his body, or because he was the unique symbol of the powers a person could embody, he became a legend: he understood the language of birds, he could speak to the wind, he made the djinns he vanquished gather pearls and coral from the seas and forced captive demons to build magnificent palaces. Perhaps this was the only way he could forget the unfortunate circumstances of his conception, by girding himself from head to toe in miracles. Solomon's inevitable fate, however, was to become a vassal to his own might.

Right now, he's fulminating over Belkis, the Queen of Sheba. Belkis, who is on her way to surrender bloodlessly to him, and has sent her most precious belongings; but her tributes are paltry amid Solomon's pompous regency. Fists clenched, he bellows at the top of his lungs. The more he looks at the diamond-filled chests and ruby-crusted daggers, the more enraged he becomes.

"How am I to take pride in these? Is she giving out alms?!" he yells over and over again.

Though he grumbles that these gifts make a mockery of his power, his irritation is not so much at a queen having consented to becoming his subject, as at a woman giving herself up without a fight. His anger is less the fury of a king than it is the peevishness of a lover. He decides he must do something to charm this Belkis, to conquer this impertinent, sun-worshipping woman without bringing her to her knees. His dignitaries are bowed like commas. Nobody knows what to say. You're there, too, standing behind his messengers, watching as everything unfolds. Watching the light saturate and refract off the marble floor, you can't help but regret having left your camera at home. There and now, are you someone else? Are you Solomon, whose grizzled beard quivers as he yells, or are you Belkis, tied by your belly to the sun?

The leopard trembles. Solomon turns to his aides with an imperious air.

"Who can bring Belkis's throne to me before she arrives?"

In that moment, your heart begins to swell, Solomon's passion pulses in your veins. You feel like that stately king, your mouth bone-dry with unease. You, more than any other, believe in the possibility of this impossible request. You're on the verge of slipping past Solomon's messengers and throwing yourself before him. But a goat-eyed little man acts before you can. His face is ruddy, his cheekbones exceedingly high: Zekvan, Solomon's most talented demon. Zekvan steps forward, clasps his hands on his stomach, and kneels respectfully.

"I will bring Belkis's throne," he says, "and what's more, I'll do it before your majesty rises from his."

You hate this answer, telling yourself it's too late, far too late. The time it would take for Solomon to rise from the throne would be as protracted as the time it must have taken for the leopard on his back to be born, to join a pack, for it to be felled by the arrow of a sharpshooter as it chases after deer, for its skin to be stripped and dried, for that skin to be stitched by the nimble hands of the royal tailor until it finally swathed Solomon's shoulders. And you know that a fleeting moment in a dream can dilate, expand, slow. It's not enough to be quick. One would have to bend time for the sake of Belkis's throne. One would have to take the image reflected in Belkis's irises and place it before Solomon. One would, for instance, have to offer up to Solomon the singular moment when the evening light filtering through the windows has washed her room in the color of stone, the moment when Belkis looks upon her mother-of-pearl throne, when she is afflicted by the fear of losing it. And so, as you dream within your dream of being Belkis, a tall, slim, weary man with deep purple bags under his eyes emerges from among the king's aides. He's tired of living; his is the haggardness of having been alive for centuries, since the time of Zulqarnayn. Standing before the king, Hızır lowers his head arrogantly.

He says, "In the time it will take your majesty to blink, I will have brought to you the throne of Belkis."

Come on, wake up. Wake up… You can't bear to become Hızır.

I envy your vitality. Especially that delicate body of yours, provisional on this earth. Every time you awaken, you shimmer in the white-heat beauty of the hope that you've been born again elsewhere; you look around yourself, your eyelids swollen, confounded by the imaginal realm that dwells between dream and reality. You become a fruit rid of its peel, a honeyed thing, ready to be bitten into. But as soon as you swallow the first spit of your wakefulness, your body is overcome with resentment, discontentment with the world.

You're even more disillusioned than you used to be: your shoulders sag, your fists clench involuntarily. You can barely stand the cooing of the pigeons from the roof. I can't understand you, you the light of my eye, I simply can't understand. Why can't I convince you that I called you into this world? You are my lot in life, you are my touch, my appetite. So why am I a wound, intensified in your absence? My nose is perpetually filled with the smell of burning, and I am scorched by every fire you tend.

—

While you spent last night chasing after the dancing

man with your camera, I was cleansed by the flame. After the concert, everyone clustered around the fire burning in the square. I watched you through the flames. You were stuck in the front row of the crowd. Though their pushing made you uneasy, you stayed steadfast as you hurriedly changed the lens. You paid no heed to the twinned quivering of the blue and yellow flames, splitting the night in two, nor to the whistling that floated from the fire's heart. They say a whistling fire means a stranger will visit your house; I suppose you had already found your visitor. He stood before you as that dancing man, the very epitome of vitality. Even before you had laid him out on the flat surface of a photograph, you knew deep down that he carried in his body the spirit of the image you wanted, waiting for you in his deepest parts, and though you knew it would remain inaccessible to you, your eyes were glued to him all the same. Photographing him would be as impossible as photographing Hızır.

While the men jumped over the fire, whispering the last of their wishes to Hızır, you waited for the dancing man to take his turn, finger on the trigger, your light and speed settings ready. The spectators maintained a tempo with their applause between each jump and, as each of the jumpers drew back intuitively, they erupted in a thunderous acclaim that resounded across Ahırkapı. After a while, crossing the fire became like diving into the ocean. The whole ceremony was a kind of baptism by fire. Those brave enough to jump lined up, imposing their own order on the chaos. The dancing man was among them. As he approached the fire, step by step, even I got a little excited. He really was such a handsome man. I began to perceive, I think, what it was you saw in him: a forceful charisma that prevailed over every moment of his life. He was entirely present, in mind, in body, in past and future, in dazzling totality; as stone can be nothing more than stone, he was everything of, and nothing more than, himself...

The tempo of applause grew faster. The dancing man smiled gleefully. His gaze was fixed directly on the coals, as if in defiance of them. He took a step back and then a few steps more, threw himself with all his might at the fire, and was instantly frozen in a piercing image.

You had captured him.

His pose made him look like he was running upon the flames as they licked the hems of his pants. His neck was bent forward, tense, and his arms swung behind him. He hung in the air, on the same plane as the sparks passing into the night; with the crimson light that struck him from underneath, he was glowing as red as a coal flung from the fire. In your well-timed photograph, you had found a striking detail for us to take in. His palms were spread open. With an ordinariness that was astonishing, this gesture epitomized his familiarity with the flames. The way he submitted himself to the fire belied none of the tension that the others had felt while performing this dangerous task. The camaraderie he had with the fire was, in the fullest sense of the word, magnificent.

I had never before seen your face like that. The dancing man's soft hands caressing the flames' tongues had dispelled your ineffable anxiety. It wasn't satisfaction nor even pride that shone in your eyes; it was a stillness, an inexplicable peace of mind. The camera in your hand hung toward the ground, and in that moment, I wanted to pass through the flames and come to you. A place had opened up on your face, one where I could seek refuge.

I don't know how long I hung in the air. Although the bed of flames I crossed was no more than the length of two men, I felt like I had crossed the Red Sea. To tell the truth, the fire's red-hot scorch felt impossibly familiar. I was unfazed by the singeing of my hair. Smoked by the fire, I made four wishes to Hızır. Burn me, I asked, that I might be unrecognizable by my ashes. Accustom me to not understanding, that I might not move heaven and earth in order to know. Purge me of my languor, that I might be scorched to purity. Don't let me become the zealot of someone else's faith.

When I finally landed on the ground, you were gone. In your place was someone unexpected, a man with pitch-black eyes, his hair soaked with sweat, his leather jacket draped over one shoulder. Behind me, smoke; before me, the familiar smell of a stranger. The dancing man held his hand out to me. And I took it. There was no bone in his thumb.

We left Ahırkapı together, hand in hand, each growing quickly accustomed to the way the other walked. There was no need to say a single word as we wove our way through the crowd as a single body. The smells of the festivities came to an end once we reached the road along the waterfront. We breathed deeply, cleansing our charred lungs. Our eyes, still dazzled by the hostile glare of the spotlights, slowly purified as they took in the darkness of the Marmara. The breeze coming from the sea made us tremble from head to toe, driving us together. We were neither lovers, nor friends, nor even acquaintances. We were two strangers who nobody noticed, growing closer to each other.

There were others apart from us along the waterfront. Those who shunned the swarming throngs above gathered in small groups, continuing the celebrations on their own. Families eating cookies and drinking tea, a few old men who had set up a small table for drinks, some girls crunching on sunflower seeds; they had all called Hızır to the water. There was also a hunched old woman, at least as out of place as we were. She had filled the pocket of her wool vest with pebbles and was throwing them into the water one by one, blowing a wish on each pebble. That night, she had come in hopes of meeting Hızır, in hopes of swapping the grievous weight of all her pains for gratitude. We passed her slowly, trying not to draw her attention. The sound of the pebbles striking the sea resounded in my ears.

The closer we got to Sarayburnu, the farther I drew away from the living monuments of the present tense. Every grievous pebble the old woman threw into the sea conjured in her mind an image of her younger self, each equipped with senses and faculties, disappearing as soon as the next pebble spirited up the next version of herself, and as the maudlin moments amassed on the seafloor, a present tense came into being, soaking wet and undone by the past. The present that would never come to be resided solely in her body, the body of a breathing, pulsing mortal, her cells disintegrating day by day. The pebbles, too, held in her liver-spotted, wrinkled hand, belonged to an earlier time.

As I dwelled on the impossibility of her present tense, my companion stopped and gestured at the lighthouse towering over the fortress walls. He began telling me of its construction, as though describing something that had taken place only yesterday. Apparently, there had once been an accident in Kumkapı. In 1700-something, after Hacı Kaptan's galley got stuck in the shallows on its way to Egypt, Osman III, sultan at the time, personally interceded to right the upturned boat. He decided to build the Ahırkapı Lighthouse, which would illuminate the waters of the Bosphorus for six seconds at a time. My companion explained that Osman III was an especially paranoid man. He had been locked in a room of the palace until his teenage years out of fear that his brother might kill him; as a consequence, open spaces made him nervous, and whenever he heard an unexpected sound, he would turn to look in that direction. Even the rustling wing of a seagull taking flight made him jump, sounding to him like a threat on his life. As if his anxieties about mortality weren't grave enough, his fear of being killed made him so excessively sensitive to sound that music and the sound of women's voices became especially unbearable. He avoided his harem to keep from hearing women. And, for some reason, he wore iron shoes. Now that he had established some kind of correlation between sound and death, every step of his iron heel raised such a clamor that he believed he could strike terror into any executioner who might be waiting in ambush. Perhaps, too, those shoes were a way for him to sense his own vitality, to feel himself truly alive. Nonetheless, his

nervous state of mind had settled itself so thoroughly
in his Constantinople that in the second winter of his
ascent to the throne, the waters of the Golden Horn
froze over, buried beneath a deep silence. You could
cross from one bank to the other on foot. That sinister winter when the water was silent had hardly been
forgotten when Istanbul was struck by two great fires
that reduced the city to ashes. In the age of Osman
III, then, water and fire both lost their temper. As the
mosques, the hamams, the mills, the beautiful neighborhoods of Istanbul were burning to the ground, my
companion had passed through those flames. In other
words, his kinship with fire reached back a very long
time.

—

I'm out of line for telling you all of this, I know.
Perhaps my words destroy the photograph you took
of the dancing man leaping over the fire. Perhaps I'm
undermining your desire to render all the bewilder-
ments of your life in images, without the need for
language. But I wouldn't have gone on this journey if
you weren't the way you are, I wouldn't have had the
audacity to chase after Hızır. Who knows how many
Hızırs there are in your imagination, Hızırs you've
insisted upon finding, no matter what, Hızırs you've

insisted upon mythologizing, upon stitching into the fabric of the world; and yet, one of them appeared to me last night. If only you knew what he told me. Until he came to you, this Hızır had gone every day of the week to one of his old stomping grounds, the mosque in Çemberlitaş, where so many servants gathered at the door of the almshouse; so many lunatics, imagining the mosque's vaulted domes to be the vaults of heaven, hoping to be raptured; so many sultans burning for worldly erudition; so many saints, hoping, through their penance, to pay the price for the blessing of divine wisdom; all sighing "Hızır, Hızır," as they stared into emptiness. They perpetually called him to their sides, as if beseeching a god who had abandoned them. Sultan Mehmed the Conqueror, for example, had a spherical gold chandelier hung in the cupola of the Hagia Sophia to indicate that this place was the seat of Hızır so that, if Hızır existed, he would sanctify the Sultan's conquest of Constantinople by making that place his earthly abode. In so doing, he hoped that Hızır would blur the sharp line between conquering the city and serving it.

Contrary to popular belief, Hızır always appears when he's called. He leaps from epoch to epoch, sidling in among people without making himself known, appearing not only in his guises of strength, but in so many other semblances. In truth, everyone sees Hızır, but nobody recognizes him. Once upon a time, for example, Sultan Suleiman the Magnificent disguised himself as a commoner and boarded a boat from Salıpazarı to the Bosphorus. Just as the boat was about to embark, your Hızır bounded onto the boat as a dapper young man. Suleiman looked suspiciously at the boy, sizing him up from head to toe. As they made their way toward Kuruçeşme, the two kept sneaking glances at each other, both in disguise, each a semblance covering up the original: an old man with a grizzled beard eye to eye with a callow young man. One appeared in his youth; the other appeared in old age. And yet, whatever curiosity Hızır wanted to live out by transforming into a young man was identical to the curiosity the sultan had in appearing as a commoner. They were not simply sitting face to face: they had traded places. It's like sometimes when you stare at someone you reflexively begin to mirror them, becoming their twin: that was how Suleiman transformed into Hızır, and Hızır into Suleiman, there in that boat. The oars seemed to grow heavier in the boatswain's hands.

At one point, Suleiman stuck his hand into the sea and caressed the water for a long time. His eyes glazed over, his body become impossibly light: his entire existence condensed into the small wetness of his palm. The water made him feel like he was neither sultan nor old man any longer. He didn't even realize that the ruby ring he wore on his little finger, a keepsake of his mother Hafsa Hatun, had slipped off into the water. When he realized the loss, he said nothing; lamenting a piece of jewelry was unbecoming of a sultan. But then, something unexpected happened. As they approached the dock in Kuruçeşme, that callow young man stuck his hand in the water and produced a ruby ring. Suleiman, still disguised as an old man, took the ring and placed it on his finger. When the young man climbed onto land and disappeared, Suleiman was confronted by a paradox. Perhaps his anxiety about losing the ring had made him imagine a Hızır in the face of that young man. Or perhaps the youth had transformed into Hızır, just for a moment, and taken the ring back from the sea.

I don't know which of these two alternatives Sultan Suleiman decided upon. Since I heard this story from the mouth of Hızır, I have no choice but to take him, the young man who pulled the ring from the ocean, at face value. But right now, as you stand in the shower washing yourself, everything I'm saying feels meaningless.

—

Hot steam rises up between us. We've become separated from each other by a veil of water droplets. You're not rinsing yourself in the water, but offering yourself up to it. I can hardly make out the redness of your eyes, the sagging of your tired muscles. Nor can I hear the covenant you're pledging to the water. You feel your words, drop by drop, upon your translucent skin. Standing there under the water, unmoving for minutes on end, you let the water take the shape of your body, confiding yourself to the droplets, one by one, until your every cell is soaking wet. At moments like these, I desire you even more, your face softening with a deep calm, your blurry reflection in the sweaty mirrors a shadowy creature, as if the dirty bubbles that leave streaks on the glass, as if the strands of hair gathering in the drain, are not traces of you but of someone else. You cleanse everything, your inside, your outside, your cells, your time, your space, your cuticles, your future your past your life. You've managed to exclude me from that secret covenant you have with water, which hurts me deeply but also charms me. In my eyes you become a distant lover, perpetually out of reach. If only you could teach me all you've gleaned from water, if only we could speak in that language, if only we weren't stuck telling stories like this one.

I watched Hızır closely last night out of the corner of my eye. He kept brushing his hair back to keep his forehead from sweating, continuously straightening the collar of his leather jacket, trying to get it to sit right. Nothing about him expressed the exhaustion of life without end. Nor did I see in him even a trace of your ambition for reincarnation. Your fantasies about the endless recursions of life and death, beginning with your most distant ancestor, bewildered at the edge of a lake, watching rings form and spread on its surface, continuing with your distant predecessors, the ones who played the saz, and culminating finally in your grandmother Bese, born to a leatherworker who etched what he saw into strips of shagreen: all these fantasies began to waste away, evanescent as the waves churning in the Marmara on that cool May night. Fantasy is a dangerous game. You are as poetic when you daydream as you are prosaic when you fantasize. You draw darkness into yourself, as if inhaling nonexistent air. The outer world of figs and olives and grapes, all the images of this world reflected in your mind, come undone in the realm of your fantasies. If you hadn't insisted so much on Hızır, reincarnation could have been such a beautiful dream. If you hadn't abused yourself in this way, you could have been content with who you are without Hızır, you could have hardened yourself to the shame you inherited. The same is perhaps true for other things too...

—

Over the course of our stroll along the water, I told Hızır a story of reincarnation for the sole purpose of provoking him. Assailing him in this way was my only chance to reach you. The more I spoke, the slower Hızır walked. Eventually, he came to a complete stop, looking me in the face as he listened to my words. Under the streetlights, his eyes seemed full of melancholic unease. I told him about the young architect Isidore, recalling what I'd read in *The Extinct Times of Byzantium*, which explains in meticulous detail how the Hagia Sophia was built, how it was damaged by the earthquakes that leveled Constantinople, and how its magnificent sanctuary was constructed anew. In 558, after an earthquake, the apse collapsed. The young architect, named in honor of his uncle who had built the cathedral, wandered for days amid the rubble, trying to figure out how to rebuild the sanctuary more durably to withstand the next earthquake. Isidore instinctively believed that every mistake held a truth waiting to be discovered. Having come of age working as an apprentice to his uncle, his inherited knowledge was insufficient; he had to conjure up the missing knowledge himself. Repairing the Hagia Sophia quickly became a story not of the cathedral's transcendence, but of Isidore's. Several days later, Isidore finally discovered why the dome hadn't held against the earthquake; its construction was too broad, practically an ellipse, and the scaffolding had been removed while the mortar was still damp. Based on the calculations he did, the dome had to be raised six and a half meters in order to sit securely. As the young architect in the story wandered among the rubble, searching for unbroken bricks to reuse, he discovered an astounding piece of writing. Lining up the bricks side by side revealed a long letter penned by his uncle, Isidore of Miletus. More than a letter, in fact, it was a sequence of signatures. "I am Ionian," Isidore of Miletus wrote:

> My spirit has dwelled in Ionia since creation. I was
> Atlantis, I became the Aegean, I was Pythius who built
> the Mausoleum at Halicarnassus, and I was Praxiteles
> who sculpted the Aphrodite of Knidos. I was Phidias
> who carved Zeus out of ivory, Chares who erected the
> Colossus of Rhodes; I was Chersiphron, I built the
> Temple of Artemis at Ephesus. And I was Lysippos, I
> sculpted the pure-blooded horses that haul Hercules to
> the Armageddon. Now I am Isidore of Miletus. As one
> of two architects of this sanctuary of divine wisdom, I
> fulfilled my duty when I placed the fortieth keystone of

this dome. I will die soon but I will never end, not until
I live out my reincarnations and reunite with the divine
whole which is 'one.'

You should have seen Hızır's face when I finished this
story, carried away, waxing poetic. It was clear that he
envied Isidore of Miletus's way of celebrating himself.
Seizing my opportunity, I said to him, really, I'm curious, since you were born in the era of the Prophet
Abraham, since you've watched the geographies you've
wandered take so many forms, witnessed a sea become
a river delta home to many birds, witnessed that delta
become a barren meadow, witnessed that meadow
become a village enclosed by tangerine orchards, witnessed the village grow into a city, witnessed the ruins
that replaced the city, how is it that you can bear to
watch the pure world tend toward destruction, as, for
example, when you appeared before Bese dressed as a
junk collector? How have you endured thousands of
years marred by the cruelty of pharaohs, brutal plagues
and massacres and slavery, the tears of a weeping child
whose arm was blown off in a minefield? Ultimately,
you are human. You were welcomed to Bese's dinner
table because of your humanity, because you are able
to weep. You could have allayed her inveterate sense of
loss, if only for a moment, before the profound silence
of God. But perhaps, by appearing as a junk collector,

all you did was deepen the chasm of her spellbinding loss. So I have to wonder, what good did your visitation do? Are you the face of an anxiety for which holy books, angels, spirits, and djinns, the world-weariness of a pious woman with a predilection for the supernatural, are not enough? Or perhaps, Hızır, are you longing incarnate? Are you the brothers who disappear, the husbands whose corpses are never found, the sons who leave and never return?

He didn't like what I said, of course, and scowled at me, nudging my shoulders gently, directing me toward the water. We sat on the large rocks just beyond the concrete pathway. The night had grown silent. The cars passing on the avenue behind us were now few and far between, and the whole city had been enveloped in the delicate murmuring that rose ceaselessly from the sea. The earth seemed perfectly horizontal. Imagine that all the heights in our field of vision, all the freighters waiting in the ocean, had plunged into darkness, that we sat on the same plane as the lights burning on the opposite shore: I felt like we were on a very flat tray, the vaulted sky enfolding us. In spite of the open air and the cool breeze, a malaise overtook me. I felt like I had been ensnared. I couldn't budge from my place, even if I wanted to; I couldn't come to you, so long as I wasn't called.

Feeling stifled, I thought about the last time you saw your grandmother, a year before she died. The poor woman had already grown so weak due to her kidneys. She kept the two kidney stones she had passed, wore them like jewels around her neck. Whenever anyone would ask her, how are you?, how do you feel?, she would show them the stones resting between her breasts. They were no longer mere lopsided stones but the manifestation of her sorrow, wordless stories she had knit together, particle by particle, with the dust that accumulated in her groin. These jewels had torn her apart as she cast them out of her body; displaying them like this was her way of saying everything there was to say without breaking her silence. That day, as she stirred the porridge in her copper cauldron she let out a long sigh. Lately, every remembrance of hers was accompanied by such a sigh. Then a strange, unexpected sentence slipped out of her mouth.

"There's no such thing as leaving... there's only being called."

You were reclining on the divan. Perhaps Bese had forgotten your presence and was only speaking to herself. You sat up slowly, without making a noise. Your grandmother was weeping. What's more, she was weeping for you. You didn't know what to say.

"Being called?"

"Nobody goes anywhere if someone doesn't call them, nobody moves a muscle if they're not called somewhere."

You stood up and embraced your grandmother from behind. Your twenty years were too few to understand what she wanted to say, but you pretended anyway, caressing her white hair. This tiny woman, whose death was close at hand, about to fall, about to slip through your fingers and leave. Finding solace in your warmth, she raised her head and began to shout.

"Ah!" she said, "But whoever called my İlyas away, may his hands be broken, may his tongue fall out of his mouth, may his two eyes melt out of his head!"

Leaving is a grievous thing. Especially when you're the one staying behind, watching someone go, your last image of them the hard lines of their back. The soles of their feet, visible with every step, now seem to tread toward darkness, toward the empty land of the beyond. Yet the same grasses grow in every corner of the world. And so, just as the one left behind must suffice unto themselves, the one who leaves makes their way toward themselves. Nobody introduces themselves as someone who has gone. What does "gone" mean, after all, except the human void, the bed that always still smells of skin, which holds a place among those left behind?

But there is a loss you know quite well, one that can't be compared with the loss of a place or a relative. It's an age-old story, to be spirited away like the tortuous, ongoing romance between predator and prey; this is a story of how you were seized by beauty. The summer you went on holiday to Kaş, when you stepped out from under the blue tarp awning and plunged into the water, you were inevitably going to get lost. You had a snorkel in your mouth. All you could hear was your own breath and the lapping of the sea. You'd swum toward the rocks, your body parallel to the realm of the sea, entirely outside of vertical life. First, a school of bream passed beneath your stomach. You watched them calmly congregate on the surface of the water to feed. At the slightest movement of your hands, though, the fish darted like arrows in every direction, and you, too, traced a winding course through the water. You were not going anywhere, not heading in any direction, only being carried away.

I was inside you then. Your pulse had accelerated. With every stroke you took, the threads tacking me to you grew taut, and I felt the needling heat of the sun on my back. You couldn't swim as fast as the bream, of course, but you noticed an enormous fish hidden among the scallops, black with bulbous eyes and a large lower jaw. It withdrew beneath the rocks. That was where, amid the sea urchins, you saw the stingray. It covered almost the entire surface of the rock, and resembled a book, its pages fluttering back and forth, as it swam. Its skin was so white it was practically transparent; you could almost see the configuration of its bones. There was a suspicious calmness about it. It didn't swim, really, but flowed through the water. It was a dreamlike being, unfeeding, unbreathing, even unliving. After seeing the ray, you disappeared. Truly, you disappeared. You were no more than a human body reflecting it. Eventually, the water's temperature began to change and the seafloor grew dark. Once you lost track of the ray, you released yourself to the water in order to rest. Except for your spine, you had gone soft all over, all your joints loose. Your jaw ached from biting down on the snorkel's mouthpiece. Then the ray sprung up again. Or was it a different one? It must have been bigger, more beautiful, than the first one. For some reason you wanted to believe it was the same ray. You had kept the covenant between you and the ray even from yourself.

We stayed on the surface of the water for a long time in pursuit of the new ray. Such extraordinary things we saw: turquoise stones, sunken minarets sheathed in limestone, enormous sea snails, bony marine plants setting their roots free in the sand... As the water grew colder, the colors below changed, and the sea creatures grew larger and larger in size. Eventually, this ray disappeared, too; in any case, you no longer had the energy to swim. When you lifted your head above the water and removed your snorkel, you were struck with fear.

What you saw was this: the bay dotted with blue tarps where you had gotten in the water was gone, and you found yourself in the middle of a large U-shaped bay, a different one, surrounded with olive trees. As the rose-hued sky darkened rapidly into night, you couldn't figure out where you were, or which direction you should swim in. You swam out of that bay and into the open waters. Your lips were numb from the salt, your body temperature had plummeted, and you trembled like a leaf. The sea had swathed you in all its violence. This other bay, no bigger than a matchbox, was completely empty, no towels fluttering in the breeze, no splashes deflecting off other swimmers' bodies. It was a terrifying thing, this unpeopled place, a terrifying solitude. The ray that called you into the open waters offered itself as the means to measure the distance to your origin. The frontier of your disappearance began where the ray had been awaiting you.

There in the middle of the sea, I saw an ancient memory flash up in your terror-filled eyes. You were so alive then, so rudely awakened to the possibility of being left suddenly alone there, alone in the unknown. At the same time, your whole body, from head to toe, was the kernel of a cosmic loneliness. Losing yourself meant becoming lost in yourself. Opposite, a sea, in the sea a devil, a devil disguised in the beauty of a ray, you lured by the ray, then a weary body, and another hidden body fighting off the fear of death: one by one, you multiplied. You knew now the dangers not only of being called, but of calling. One should not confront another like this, disguised in the beauty of a ray...

Perhaps because Hızır and I were silent for such a long time that night, sitting on the rocks in Sarayburnu, I grew calm as we looked out upon the uniform hue of the sea, its utter motionlessness violating the laws governing the boundless sky, and the feeling of suffocation constricting my throat began to abate. The quietude between Hızır and me was so much more than the silence and suppressed condemnations that Bese left you: it was a plane where words failed to be words; or rather, it was a crystal-clear depth, a wordless plane where no single word found its place. All I felt was the pressure of the air as I shifted my weight from my left hip to my right. I was cradled in a fervor woven of silk, and breathed in the air not with lungs but with gills, tasting the perfection of happiness, there on the threshold of a pure desire purged of eroticism. It was a tranquility I can't possibly administer to you. The most I could do would be to etch into your spirit all the trembling reflections of light on the Marmara. The rest was left only to me, an indivisible globe of tranquility.

Hızır was naturally outside of this globe. I realized he wasn't entirely there beside me when I broke the silence and turned my head towards him. He was there, a young man listening to the night with me, and he was Poseidon who taught Odysseus the wrath of the Black Sea. Not merely content to wander endlessly through parallel universes, to leap from time to time, he also cast himself from name to name. Hızır was called in every direction. An abundance of Hızırs sat there next to me, each snarled in the involutions of time by the chain linking his many incarnations. There was the time he turned into two people at once, split into the two bodies of Elijah and Elisha, the Hebrew prophets who wandered the banks of the River Jordan. From where I sat I watched these two friends bidding fond farewells to one another. Elijah was distraught at the state of the world, while Elisha had become mute, utterly silent out of a fear of being alone. Elijah beseeched Elisha: "ask something of me before I go." Elisha replied in a tremulous whisper: "two parts of your spirit would be enough." Elijah mounted a horse of fire, which had descended from the heavens; Elisha took two breaths, inhaling the emptiness left behind. While Elisha watched in infinite sadness as his closest friend departed, elsewhere, Hızır used rope to secure a boat and its crew caught in a storm in the Mediterranean, and still elsewhere, Khwaja Khizr saved a little girl drowning in a river in Bengal. The very moment he pulled the girl from those ferocious waters, he sat in the shade of a cypress

tree, chatting with Şeyhülislam Yahya Efendi outside a
dervish lodge in the Yıldız district of Constantinople,
and as their conversation reached its height, he became
the Prophet Idris, muttering to himself as he sewed
in his workshop, when he heard a woman singing a
hymn to honor Raja Jindar, wandering the length of
the canals surrounding the emerald rice fields on the
island of Bali, and just as he was swept up in the words
of the song, he appeared and disappeared as the martyr
Ali among the Nusayris in Syria, yet at the same time
he was in the hearts of the Uighurs as the sage named
Göksakal. Before he had the name Utnapishtim, and
began describing, to Gilgamesh, the locus of the cov-
eted plant of youth, he was Saint George, the stoic
sufferer who was cut into pieces, and joined in the
celebrations of the rites of spring in Constantinople.
As he sat on the twelfth fur in a Bektashi Lodge, he
suddenly appeared in Khorasan as an old man dressed
in a white cape, gave directions to a lost peddler, and
from there became the wise man Ea, watching the
hands of a skilled sculptor in Babylon rendering Enki,
the Sumerian Water God, standing upon a large fish.
When he was Glaucos, King of Corinth, slicing open
his enemy's chest in the Trojan War, he was simultaneously a spirit enveloping Mesopotamia, he was Helios
shouldering the sun, Dumuzid who arranges to marry

Inanna, the Raa Haq in Dersim, and a hungry beggar who came to Bese's table.

Hızır was the immortal figure of the east, weaving a web across time. He was a pair of eyes that always watched from afar, when the heart didn't beat strongly enough and hope began to fade. He was neither saint nor prophet nor angel, nor even really a sage, and much less was he a god; yet he was all of these at once. He chose to appear in times of extreme difficulty and debilitating indigence, in places where death made its rounds. Perhaps Hızır's gaze was merely a proxy for God to bear witness to this calamitous world. He wandered this earth as a body incognito, carrying the secret purpose of all things past and future like a seed inside himself. He was a being whose every action held some meaning, who evoked the unspeakable without saying a word, who alluded to the unerring causality at the core of every coincidence.

I couldn't bring myself to turn to Hızır and beg for the truth, couldn't muster the courage to ask, where were you in 1938? Do you see now a wounded people, fleeing from Dersim to the Black Sea? Is there a girl sitting by the fire, her eyes the color of olives? Were you truly there when Bese wandered into the forest? And if not you then who, who appeared before Bese, a devil disguised in beauty, and called her to him?

"By the fig and the olive," begins the Surah At-Tin, "We have created man in the best of stature." God, in other words, swears upon the fig. For the Creator to have sworn upon the name of one of his creations… it's a magnificent figure of speech. God speaks not with the voice of Gabriel but with the voice of humankind. And with the voice of humankind, which encompasses all realms of creation, He honors the fig.

But I've never heard you swear upon the fig, in spite of all the intimacy you feel for it. You've never made Zevraki bear witness to an oath, and even when you begged it to bear fruit, you never kneeled before it like it was a god. Nor have you ever called someone you love by that name, "my fig." But now, seeing the way you gently dry your naked body, it seems impossible to praise you with anything but the fig. If I were to speak in a voice stolen from you I would love you only by way of the fig. The way your knees bend as you dry your calves; the way you lean back nonchalantly when you sit; the way your hands move at random; every little gesture calls to mind the incidental beauty of the fig hanging from its branch. In the ordinary yet austere way your spine curves, I can see that mysterious singularity that everyone possesses, the same singularity that you try to capture in your photographs. Your back forms a new arc. When you bend down, your round stomach protrudes, that hidden globe beneath your ribs leaping out of you. You must be rather round. You hide yourself in your belly. When you're naked, the sharp angles your joints form instantly give up their dominion.

And your breasts; ah, your breasts. You saved the right one for love, the left for emptiness. They sit far from each other due to your tenacious infertility. Your left side is less sensitive for this reason: it's insouciant to the love on the right, as firm as a green fig that sees no sun. It's almost as if no blood circulates there, in the breast that nurses the fear in your heart, which grieves prematurely for its prodigal son.

In the same way that your left breast has complied with Bese's curse ever since you became a woman, so, too, you have turned a blind eye to all the fig trees in the world because of the one you named Zevraki. In fact, whenever you enter the shade of that tree out there and pretend that it's Zevraki, under the force of an ideal that implicates every single fig, you are clinging to a being that simply doesn't exist. I don't really know how to explain it, how to explain to you that conjecture is itself a measure of the world.

There once was a man, a man who loved his wife

so much that he had a garden built for her, filled with rare black roses. There in that garden, the woman slowly began to fade away. Because every time her husband kissed her, he would whisper into her ear, you are more beautiful than all of these roses. He would go even further, in fact, pointing at the North Star, saying, you are more beautiful than this star, than that flowing river, than this butterfly, than that peacock. At her husband's words, the wife grew weaker, losing her strength daily. First, she was afflicted with jaundice, and he nursed her himself. Still, he persisted, you're more beautiful than all the fruits of this earth. When she at last recovered and was able to stand again, he brought her a stark white dove and told her, you're more beautiful than this dove. This time she was taken by consumption, and soon she was no more than skin and bone.

"Bastard," she said to him right before she died, "Even Simurgh, herself, bird of legend, was only equivalent to thirty birds. The only thing more beautiful than a dove is oblivion. Beyond black roses, there is nothingness. Even the peacock has an ugly call to attune itself to this crude world. So why do you keep reducing me to ashes? There's an entire universe swirling inside me, but you would rather have me cast into the hell of impossible perfection, of all those things I can never become."

At the very least, take an oath upon the fig tree, here and now. Swear humbly, for me, that you can do magic with the real. Imagining is nothing more than striking a bargain with the heart, a technique of humane endurance that holds the present tense in its place, leavening it. Give up that habit of nullifying everything you see and remaking it with the strength of your unruly fantasies, give up on striving to have never been born. Instead of calling the fig tree in your garden Zevraki, call me "my fig" to show me you love me. And don't ever send me chasing after Hızır again.

You'll be surprised to hear this, but apparently Hızır was a blacksmith at some point on his journey. Long before he slipped into Eliha's womb, he came into the world way back in the bronze age, in the kingdom of Ugarit, a kingdom long hidden in the memory of the place now called Latakia. Last night, he spoke with longing about that city, choking up several times while he recounted his tale. The midnight air had grown chilly. He raised the collar of his jacket and crossed his arms over his chest, his shoulders trembling. I can rub your back to warm you up, I said, and he pulled away immediately. This was how I realized that he didn't like to be touched. He spoke with an irritating slowness, almost as if to spite me. Recollecting his life in Ugarit, he would go quiet for a time, then form short, curt sentences.

He had been born in that verdant kingdom, its northern boundary drawn by a dense forest littered with boulders, opening into a valley as it moved south toward the sea, a valley filled with grapevines and fig trees and enclosed by olive groves like parentheses. In those times, he was a burly, thick-armed man. From birth, he'd been endowed with a terrible strength, and he spent his entire youth in a workshop far outside this port city. When he returned to the city to sell his wares to visiting traders, the people there looked askance at his face and soldiers wouldn't allow him anywhere near the palace walls. When he wandered the narrow streets of outer neighborhoods, children would flee as soon as they saw him. This was because his body bore the scars of every copper bowl he'd made, every iron lock he'd cast. His hands and face covered in burns, he was a man consumed by fire.

"I know the pain of the ember all too well," he said in a low voice. "I have tested each and every stage of iron on my flesh, one by one, as the fire turns it from red to yellow, from yellow to white-hot."

For this reason, even though he had forged all the screws, bronze doors, and iron trestles for the king's hundred-room palace, a palace built around five courtyards, a palace which left everyone awe-struck, he was never able to set foot inside it. Others found his appearance distressing, so he would return to his workshop as soon as he finished his business in the city, and wouldn't be seen again for weeks on end. But he could never stop dreaming of the palace, seat of that rich kingdom that connected Egypt to the Hittites, and Mesopotamia to the Aegean. His curiosity about the palace stemmed from the fact that the tombs of past kings were enclosed in the present king's residency.

"To live with the dead is a form of moral conduct," he said.

To establish a connection with past lives, it seemed, one had to face the smell of bones. While some civilizations leave the bodies of their dead on hills where carrion birds build their nests, or place them like seeds in memorial graves far off from their settlements, and while in some places these bodies are publicly burned or tied to rafts adorned with flowers and then pushed out onto the water, the Ugarits lived neck and neck with their dead ancestors here on this port, this place of sheer transience; and in so doing, they built an incomparable kingdom of memory. There were hundreds of clay tablets in the palace's hidden library. Epics were etched in columns on broad tablets, delineated by engraved lines, and every important development was noted moment by moment: the last acts of the pharaoh, the offerings of the Hittites to the king of the Ugarits, every last transaction, no matter how small.

"Long ago, writing was something hollow, opened up with a fine-tipped chisel," the blacksmith said, grasping an invisible hammer with his right hand. "I used to take my hammer and chisel and carve the form of the word into sheets of clay."

"I had three vowels," he continued, brandishing three fingers as if he was going to poke me in the eyes. "While other kingdoms of the time wrote only with consonants, my alphabet had three vowels. And my script was quite legible, with brackets to separate words."

As if blacksmithing weren't enough, when he began writing, began rendering the word permanent, he became regarded as a sorcerer and was soon exiled. This unnerving artisan lived on his own, away from society, and whatever deficit he created in the kingdom of Ugarit, whatever absence was left behind when he withdrew to the comfort of his workshop, was filled by a god named Kothar.

"Didn't you get bored?" I asked. "How did you bear being alone, all by yourself?"

He replied, "The sound of the anvil strikes in the heart of the city."

Every time he struck the molten iron against his anvil, giving it shape, he attuned himself to the pulse in his wrist, to the breath in his chest, to the tentative groans coming out of his mouth, and found himself moving in ceaseless rhythm. Beating the iron against the anvil became as spellbinding as prayer, and he slowly became insensate in that rhythm, the tension in his body dissipating. In this way, he came together with far-off city dwellers, and his loneliness temporarily subsided. This litany of devotions served as the labor through which the oar-rowing sailor, the axe-swinging logger, the anvil-striking ironsmith, took part in the world with their entire being.

Sometimes this young ironworker would give up on being Kothar and go down to the shore in the garb of a porter or beggar. He would listen to the stories told by visiting traders who assembled in inns, bringing saws from Lebanon, tin from Iran, wine from Cyprus, olive oil from Mykonos, and slaves from Egypt. He would help unload ivory-inlaid chests and bales of silk from ships. He discovered from the tradesmen of nearby civilizations their ways of thinking, examined one by one the necklaces of jade, the Egyptian blue jugs made by passing glass over porcelain, the amphorae from Crete littering the market, and tried to understand how fire and water and earth could be molded by human hands. So many human qualities hidden in the skin of objects. From the pots and pans on display in the market, he learned of Egypt's ethereality, the Hittites' displays of power, the Aegean's world of pleasures.

—

One day, as he toiled in his workshop, a soldier came

to his door. The blacksmith was told that he was being commissioned to do the metalwork for a large temple being built in the city, and he bowed his head to hide his excitement.

"Bowing your head is like placing your head on the ground," he said, which I found quite strange. He must have realized it, too, because he turned and bowed respectfully to the Marmara. "To bow your head is not only to obey, but also to demonstrate that you will remain loyal to the king."

The temple's construction lasted exactly seven years. This resplendent building had no windows, and was so big that it could be seen even from the sea. It was to be the first sight on land for returning sailors, an icon to celebrate their homecoming. For those seven years, the blacksmith worked day and night. Once, as he was covering a room with a sheet of silver, he cut the thumb of his right hand. The wound was deep and turned gangrenous, forcing him to have the thumb amputated at the root. He lost his left eye to an ember that leapt out of his hearth as he prepared the star-shaped lead casts for the stones which were to decorate the temple's courtyard. One of the iron frames he built to stabilize the beams fell on his foot, and left him with a limp. His hands grew larger every day, and his beard began falling out in patches because of the burns on his face. His neck calcified under the burden of what he had to lift. His spine warped, and bumps developed between his shoulder blades. When the temple's construction finally came to an end, the blacksmith was left disfigured, a monstrosity. He was no longer allowed into the city at all, and lived the rest of his life on the quiet cliffside where his workshop was located; apart from wanderers, loggers, and women who had lost their way gathering wild grasses, he would never again feel the warmth of human company. But the Ugarit sailors never forgot his existence. At the entrance of the temple, they left anchors, sailcloths, oars, and pieces of iron, all salvaged from ships they pillaged, as oblations to Kothar.

After his life as an outcast ironworker, he presided as a god who ruled all the seas, who knew the language of minerals, who discovered music and invented writing, a weary and wounded god who wanted no sacrificial offerings, who had a distaste for pomp, who preferred testing men to punishing them, who never removed his feet from the earth…

—

"I know all too well what it means to hurt," Hızır said, "I know the searing pain of molten lead, the feeling of being completely and utterly alone, unable to hear a single voice. I know what it means to stare at lapis rocks, to beseech sunning lizards for help; I know what it means to be left breathless looking for veins of silver in the walls of a cave, to be crushed between timber flowing down a river, to break a bone, to disappear; I know what it feels like to run for your life through an impenetrable forest, entangling yourself in the underbrush at every step, scraping against poisonous plants that leave you in instant pain; I know the sudden appearance of a cat's claws, the stinging pain of being whipped by branches, the consuming thirst that drives you to suck the dew off leaves. And I know how to pity myself through my own eyes even though I have disappeared from the eyes of others."

He was going to continue, but I couldn't bear it any longer. I interrupted him: "I know all of this already."

He frowned. "How is that possible?"

"Because I remember," I said. "It's the kind of memory that

we are writing down

right now

you and I both

letter by letter."

Your photos of the Hıdrellez celebrations aren't bad at all. You're improving with each passing day. What I like most is that you see depth. Even in the scenes utterly teeming with crowds, your naturalistic gaze has managed to preserve the horizontality of the world. Your eye manages to capture the pearl in spite of the oyster. It's a simple approach, but it doesn't neglect the distance. A lighthouse fluttering in the upper corner, the red line of an ember leaping from the fire into the darkness, an orphaned hand outstretched behind the crowd, they all draw the viewer into the distance. You always manage to grasp the mystery that hides in the scene you're observing.

The dancing man really was quite photogenic. He had an air of innocence, as though he was unaware he was being watched. It's interesting, I'm just noticing now, he's the color of honey. He looks Georgian. Based on the sharp angle of his chin, I think he must have had roots in the Caucasus. Or was he actually from Istanbul? Given that he had come to the celebration on his own, perhaps he was a traveler who had stopped in the city. He might have been a tourist staying in Sultanahmet. Something about the way he gave himself so easily to the music, the way he approached so close to the fire, would suggest the excessive abandon so typical of foreigners. His exuberance was truly enviable. See here, how unabashed he is by the width of his mouth when he smiles! Unlike most of the characters you try to conjure up, there's nothing mythic about this man. Even in the picture of him leaping, the fire looks more mythic than he does. As if only the fire is aware of your gaze.

I must congratulate you, now you have another photograph of a ghost to add to your wall as a portent of death, a new face that you haunt, that haunts you. The dancing man's countenance clearly shows the attack you've waged on him. In your zeal, you seized his spirit. And though you fill your walls with all these Hızırs of your own creation, you remain an ego devoid of Hızır. You try to embody Bese's moral fortitude, but in the process, you spill outside of yourself, and in spilling you split in half, into another person, and that other person becomes a stranger, and you have no choice but to observe that stranger, always, to listen to her tortured voice.

—

In this instant, everyone is looking at you. Despite your bashfulness, you're imprisoned in our gaze. We see you from every direction: from the back of your head, from below your neck, through a magnifying glass, from afar, from the front, from the side. We're haunting you. If we were even more impudent, we would be able see you drooling from the corner of your mouth as you sleep, the way you scratch yourself here and there. Even though our gaze is directed at you, it's not the kind of gaze you can return. At most, you can try to envision yourself through our eyes, but even that would be in vain, like trying to know what it is you see in the surface of your reflection in a mirror. So instead of searching for Bese's Hızır in photographs, I wish instead that you would see Bese in your dreams, that in your sleep she might take you upon her lap and cleanse you, that her breasts, slack from nursing, hung so low they might have brushed your cheeks; or else, perhaps, that the two of you had gone on a walk in the forest, and the moment you bit into the sorrel she gave you, your hair might have suddenly grown long; or that she might have fed you bread and honey while speaking to you in a soft, low-pitched voice, saying, "Beautiful girl, little one, you must call everything by its name," and you might have awakened in a state of intoxication. If you hadn't hidden Bese in Hızır's unfathomable countenance, then we wouldn't gawk at you like this. Free from our prying eyes, perhaps you wouldn't have attempted to drag the strangers in the photographs, all those people you treat like family, into your own history of suffering.

Don't expect any help. Our gaze is merciless. We enjoy injecting ourselves with a nonfatal dose of your torment. While you tremble, alone, in the cold light of phosphorescent eyes, we stand together and keep warm. Your shame becomes a spectacle, one we simply can't resist. The fact that you're afraid of strangers, that you're suspicious of men when you walk alone, that you retreat from external suffering even as you chase after inner suffering: each, in our eyes, is the basis of a parable, a lesson to be learned.

Gouge these eyes out!

and place me on your iris.

I'm tired of speaking for you when you go silent. I've given up on watching. If you knew the hell Hızır raised for me last night you wouldn't be striking such poses for the world.

—

What if, instead, you wait for an uncle to appear, one named İlyas, and dream about being able to put an end to the cycle of that longing? Perhaps İlyas will come one day, his face, apart from a few unfamiliar lines, bearing an uncanny resemblance to your father's; you will sit across from each other in your living room, paying no heed to the faces watching from the walls, frozen in time. Drinking cup after cup of tea, he will tell you about the women he's loved, about his life as a traveling salesman, all the curious things that have happened to him in little hotels, and maybe he will even tell you about his sense of rootlessness, the way he feels like a visitor everywhere, how uneasy he has been with no hearth or home of his own, and perhaps, at this somber moment in your conversation, he will even shed a few tears. You will notice how he holds things with his fingertips, and through that detail you will try to understand all the trials and tribulations of his life.

The story of a life is always better. It is always better to chase after a long-lost uncle than after a Hızır.

Late last night, I got on a boat with Hızır. It was past three. We sat on the rocks on the waterfront until we heard the sound of the motor on a fishing boat passing nearby. Hızır stood up and gave a sharp whistle, and the sound immediately began moving toward us. The boat must have been no more than an arm's length away when the lighthouse's beam finally brought it into view, rocking calmly upon the waves, its pilot a gnarled figure, frightful as Hades. The fisherman had a look of disappointment on his face. He glanced at me, then at Hızır. We were, apparently, not the people he was hoping to find, but he hesitantly held out his hand nonetheless. I climbed aboard first, followed by Hızır, and we squeezed into the seat of the boat. The fisherman commanded the engine's rudder. His face was so disfigured with scabs that it looked like the shell of a turtle. I would be lying if I said I didn't feel uneasy; overcome with pity, I couldn't bring myself to look him in the eyes. He told us he had a hereditary condition that withered him away cell by cell; his flesh dries up and then falls off in desiccated pieces. His earlobe fell off just the other day.

"Does leprosy really still exist?" I asked, confused.

"I live in an ancient time," the fisherman replied,

smiling grimly.

The waters of the Bosphorus were nonetheless familiar, the sea as ancient as its waves. The buildings were the same, the hotels lit up in the distance, the sound of music reverberating from the nightclubs on the opposite shore, the cruise ships coming from Greece... in short, Istanbul was downright dizzy, in a state of perpetual sleeplessness. The only things out of place were we ourselves, making our way toward Galata Bridge in our cobalt-blue single-engine motorboat, leaving no ripples in the water behind us.

The fisherman told us a story. Once on another night like this, as he headed out to sea close to daybreak, he saw a silhouette moving upon the jetty near the dock at Yenikapı. If not for the burning tip of the figure's cigarette, it would have been impossible for the fisherman to make him out.

"It was pure coincidence. First I saw the cigarette and then I saw him," he told us. He redirected the boat away from the open sea, approached the jetty, and said, "Come, brother, let's go enjoy ourselves some sea air."

He scratched his head through his wool cap. "I'm a free and easy guy," he said, "not keen on formality. My door is open to everyone, there is always a vacant seat at my table, and I gladly share my cigarettes. When I'm hungry, I sit at the first table I come upon, and as soon as I'm full, I get up. Nothing in this life bothers me more than supplication. To supplicate is to ask for something with the devil's hand. First the devil gives advice, then he supplicates."

The man got on the fisherman's boat freely and easily. He was well-dressed, though he wore a scowl on his face, and looked tough, like a gangster without a gun. His shirt sported a mandarin collar; the fisherman had for some reason clung to that detail. They made their way along the coast toward Beşiktaş. It was August, a still summer night when the Marmara listens to itself, when the fish migrate in the water's deep currents toward the Black Sea. Upon their arrival to Bebek, the fisherman turned off the motor. He took out a bottle of cognac and salted nuts. The young man in gangster clothing had still not opened his mouth to say a single word, but our hero talked and talked. He unloaded his heavy heart, letting loose every sentence he had held back from others; the misery of decomposing before death, his fear of perpetual bachelorhood, all the sources of shame that he had never revealed to a single soul.

"Talking to him that night, I was cleansed," the fisherman said. "I became as light as a feather."

He must have drunk his cognac too quickly. His

face burned in searing pain with every word. Just before dawn was about to break, when *the sky whose creator I beseech* began to descend in harlequin color upon the waters, he saw a crowd of people rushing around on the waterfront of Bebek Park. One figure carried a giant spotlight, another carried a silver reflector panel as tall as he was, and behind them, was a man with a movie camera… It turned out they were filming a television show there. After watching them awhile, the fisherman started the motor and steered away. First, they went to Anadolu Hisarı, eating egg and potatoes and drinking cognac on the dock with the other fishermen. The man dressed as a gangster still hadn't spoken one word.

"I have the utmost respect for silent men," the fisherman said, lowering his voice; in his opinion, staying silent was a sign of patience. In the end, he left the young man in Beşiktaş. The young man gave him a lot of money as they bade farewell. "Please don't misunderstand, I'm not telling you this so you'll give me money. But that man came to me like Hızır in my time of need," he said, and I quickly glanced at Hızır. The fisherman's story didn't seem to have much effect on him; he'd listened not with contempt but with indifference.

We were passing underneath Galata Bridge when

the fisherman silenced the motor, and we found ourselves in a different soundscape, surrounded by hordes
of flapping seagulls, their harsh cries resounding in
our minds. The fisherman adopted an enigmatic air
as he told us the next part of his story. Ten days after
his encounter with the young man, he was at home
one evening, his children watching television, when
something had caught his eye. There was a scene on
the television of an argument in Bebek Park. The
man grabbed the woman by her shoulders and shook
her, saying "If I leave you here, it's all over." She'd
replied with something banal like, "If you don't leave
now, we'll never get past this." It was, of course, a
complete mystery as to why they were saying these
things to each other, dressed to the nines in a park in
the middle of the night. The actor wore a chic jacket
with three buttons. His collar was a mandarin collar.

The fisherman had thrown himself in front of
the television. "I know this guy, but how?" He had a
scowl on his face, his shave was so clean it looked like
it'd been drawn by a ruler; he looked like a lowlife
and a gentleman at the same.

"Holy shit!" he said, smacking his knee. "The guy
I took on my boat was an actor!"

While watching the ridiculous bickering of the
man and the woman near the dock in Bebek Park, the

fisherman saw a blue boat passing in the background, floating silently within the frame of the television box. It was him on the boat, and across from him, a well-dressed young man… at last he saw how drunk he had been. His face was beet red and his scaly nose, on the verge of falling off, was even more swollen than usual. From afar, his neck looked exceedingly thin, and his head swayed back and forth like an empty squash dangling from a trellis. The young man was in two places at once: the actor in the park and the passenger listening attentively to the fisherman, his hands tucked between his legs. The two deadlocked lovers arguing in the foreground, a boat disappearing into the distance in the background, a blemish on the sunrise.

"I was stupefied after that," the fisherman said, his voice trembling. "I couldn't believe anything I saw anymore."

Ever since that August night, the fisherman has been setting out to sea at the same time almost every night, looking for that man on the shores of the Bosphorus. At one point, he touched me and Hızır with his gnarled hands. He touched us almost combatively, as though to compensate for his fear, in order to gauge with his unfeeling fingers whether or not we were real. I couldn't say a thing, and Hızır had deliberately gone quiet. The fisherman knit his brow, presuming we didn't believe him. Clearly, he had never been able to convince anyone of the truth of his story. When we climbed back on land at the fish market in Karaköy, he bade us a brief goodbye, tied his ship to the dock, and went into a teahouse nearby, unable to even look us in the face. The dolor of the viscous sky began to slacken. In the new light, I could see how he dragged his left foot as he walked away from us. Hızır watched him for a long time, a compassionate smile on his face. As soon as the fisherman entered the teahouse, Hızır produced an iron rod and began to cleave a hole in the ship.

"Hey, stop it!" I cried. "What the hell do you think you're doing?!" Hızır paid me no heed, hammering the boat with all his might. As water began to seep into the floor of the boat, he leapt back on the dock, pleased with himself.

"It was a very nice boat," he said. "If I hadn't put a hole in it, two miscreants were going to come and steal it."

"What do you mean?" I said, unable to hide my bewilderment.

"Don't ask too many questions. It was not I who decided that this should happen," he replied, and turned away. Hızır didn't say another word, but he was calling me toward him. He quickly made his way into a makeshift restaurant set up under a tent beside the dock, feeling no need to look back to see whether I was following. I watched him move among the stacked tables and chairs. This was not a man walking toward his fate, but someone who challenged fate at every turn. He entered a slightly narrow street at the other end of the restaurant tent and disappeared. No matter how hard I listened, I couldn't hear his foot-steps.

Somewhere in my mind I remembered all this, remembered his resolute departure. The leprous fish-erman... the sinking of the boat... the refusal to answer direct questions... I thought and thought, but couldn't figure it out.

—

As the bow of the blue boat slowly sank into the water, I glanced around me. The Golden Horn was completely silent. Not a sound could be heard but the stirring of water and the cries of seagulls. The fountain in the middle of the Horn had not yet been turned back on. I could smell the drifters who slept on the Bosphorus ferries tied to the dock, a smell that marked the difference between home and home-lessness. Like you, I was an insomniac; I listened to the collective slumber of people who, out of sight, slept in boxes propped up against each other in all the nooks and crannies of the city, sheltering from the bitter cold. Sleep smelled like something else entirely.

The junk collectors had torn through the trash bags, leaving the unwanted detritus scattered about. I peered into the street that Hızır had entered, and realized I was at the entrance of a dark passage. It took me a long time to decide whether or not to follow him. The feral dogs distrusted my presence, began to circle around me. While you thrashed sleepless and exasperated at home, I couldn't find a place for myself to turn to. So I set off walking after Hızır, wearing out the soles of my shoes.

An irrational fear overcame me when I entered that dark street. It wasn't the darkness that shook me, but the solitude and isolation. I couldn't manage to hear my own footsteps. I was surrounded by hardware stores, their interlocking, closed grates interspersed with ordinary homes, standing alone in the listless minutes of a back-breaking life of labor. These shops, which sold door hinges and electricity counters, paints and drill bits, all the materials needed to build a home, had become the noiseless walls of an aluminum labyrinth. I thought there about the daily tumult of that labyrinth, the construction foremen and the workers smelling of paint thinner who flowed through here in the daytime, the delivery truck stopping in the middle of the road to unload goods, the incessant honking of horns, the woman wandering the alleyways looking for porcelain handles for a chest of drawers; and in that instant my existence was utterly perfunctory, as I paced amid the lack of so much life. Wandering there without you incited an intense feeling of apprehension, a feeling conferred by that lack.

—

Once up on a time, there was a Kurdish man who slept on these streets, a construction worker from the Batman region. He always introduced himself with a different name. One day he was called Şeyhmus, another day he was Mehmet. One of the few things that distinguished him was his ability to mix cement mortar. Apart from the two types of basalt found in his homeland, the smooth-surfaced masculine and the porous feminine, he couldn't recognize any rocks or minerals, not marble, nor granite, nor even calcite from Niğde. For this reason, he worked in construction sites for a very low daily wage, and at the end of the workday he would head to Perşembe Pazarı, the only place he knew in all of Istanbul. He would find an ATM booth or the entrance to a stairway and curl up to sleep there, tying an empty gourd around his foot. That gourd never left his sight. People who noticed this would ask him why he tied an empty gourd around his foot, to which he'd say, "This gourd reminds me of who I am. If I lose my gourd I'll lose myself." One day, when he awoke, the gourd was gone. Whoever had played this nasty joke on him could not possibly have been aware that, in stealing the gourd, they had stolen the ego object of Şeyhmus or Mehmet or whomever else he was. The value that the Kurdish worker accorded to the gourd, to the sound it made around his ankle as he turned in his sleep, to the essential, existential quality of that sound, was thereafter unknowable, a secret whose meaning was buried in his flesh.

Meaning is the easiest prey of all. As soon as it falls into a trap, it accustoms itself slavishly to this new home; it can even become lodged in something like a gourd. Sometimes it finds a crack to slip through, like a noxious fog corroding the truth, bringing tears to the eyes. We have been severed from one another, not by our stations in life, but by these clouds of fog that envelop us in a stupor. They make us look at everything from afar, leave us lethargic behind their veils of meaning. It is only essence, the essence of the truth beyond meaning, that sets the spirit trembling with its restless rhythm. The eye turns its gaze inward, it usurps the merit of sight. But truth roams the streets, it rolls like an empty gourd in the middle of the night, it remains perpetually elusive, a secret dwelling in its proper place.

The streets in Perşembe Pazarı glimmered with motor oil, and as I walked, I ruminated on the shape of the secret between you and me. I think it looks something like a fig: a small opening in the bottom through which to take in the spirit, a delicate husk that resembles human skin, and its most turgid form, resembling a droplet of water, when it has fully ripened but has yet to fall off the branch. A spineless totality stitching itself together with interweaving filaments. Neither membrane nor pit to split this secret into slices. Our structure is exceedingly gentle, ready to be mashed in the palm, collapsing at the slightest touch. It has no fragrance, attracting us not with our noses but with our eyes. You can't comprehend its sticky taste without chewing it in your heart. Praise and rebuke at the first bite, simultaneous. And we have pips, too. Each one hides the taste of a different root. We crack them open with words. And Hızır, he opens up from one of those pips, carries us both to the same root, the same originary terror that possesses us in the face of the sacred.

—

Listen to me, let me tell you what sort of thing that

terror is. When I saw Hızır again in front of the hardware shops in the small hours of the morning, the
sounds of the ezan had begun to multiply from minarets across the city, one muezzin's oratory echoing
over another's and resounding against the cawing
of the gulls. The cries of the muezzins, some tinny
and some clear, drew me quickly into the trajectory of time. Indigo trails unfurled in the sky. I didn't
approach Hızır this time. Instead, I maintained the
distance between us, watching him from within the
silence of shadow. In the yellow glow of the streetlights, his behavior seemed to me more than a little
suspicious. How can I explain? He was stuffing his
hands in his pockets, taking them back out, brushing the arms of his jacket, straightening his collar. I
don't know whether he was aware of my presence. He
crossed from sidewalk to sidewalk, stopping in front
of the shops one at a time, unable to decide where he
was going. I was seized by a feverish trembling when
I saw him like that; I broke out in a cold sweat, and
retreated, overcome by a black intuition of what was
soon to come. At the end of the surging cadence of
the ezan, there was a thunderous, drawn-out clamor
on the main street. Someone was slowly opening the
shutters of a shop. Hızır turned in the direction of the
sound and darted quickly into the side street past the

ceramics shops. I waited at first, apprehensive, none too eager to follow him. Then I thought of you, and I ran to follow him, as fast as I could, afraid I might never be able to come back to you unless I passed through Hızır first. When I got to the top of the street, I shrunk into the entrance of an office building, hiding where I could still watch closely. Hızır stood in front of a börek bakery, raw white fluorescent light striking his face through the window. Then a boy emerged, wearing a kitchen apron that reached his knees. He must have been eight or nine. He got to work washing the shop windows, a soapy sponge in his hand. Hızır had stepped around the corner and was watching the boy intently. The scene lasted for an eternity. The boy scrubbed the windows, clearly still overcome by grogginess; the excessive attention he devoted to the task made it seem like he was still in a dream. He was caught up in that state, as if still in fetal position, lying on a torn and tattered couch in the living room of a tiny two-bed apartment. He leapt away fearfully when he noticed the young man standing behind him. In fact, unable to control himself, he let out a small scream, before quickly regaining his composure, trying to exude an air of toughness that exceeded his age.

"Brother, you won't get any börek here at this

hour, the baker comes around seven. If you're so hungry you can't wait, go up to Tarlabaşı, the soup shops there are open."

Hızır approached the boy menacingly. "Is your name Ceysûr?"

The kid took a step back, flabbergasted. "Yes, I'm Ceysûr. Why do you ask?"

Hızır grabbed the boy by his arms and pushed him against the wall. Ceysûr barely came up to Hızır's waist. I saw his legs kick in the air as his feet left the ground. Somewhere in the recesses of my mind, I remembered this scene. It dawned on me, the memory of the bloody journey that Hızır took with the Prophet Moses, and I was utterly frozen in place, my bewilderment borrowed from Moses' eyes. Hızır held the boy by the throat, lifting him into the air and slamming his head against the wall with all his strength. I recoiled, wanting to look away from the spray of blood, trying not to hear the intermittent gurgles. There were no more than seven paces between Hızır and me, seven gradations of distance from each other, seven strata that reached from deep within the earth's core, through its crust, from the sea's surface and beyond the seventh heaven. When I opened my eyes, Ceysûr was splayed out on the ground, lifeless, covered in blood, and Hızır was walking slowly toward me, wiping the blood splatters from his face and hands with a white handkerchief. There were veils between us, layer upon layer, seven veils, veils of fog, seven tightly knit veils obscuring my sight... I saw the murderer's eyes through those seven veils.

When Hızır took his first step toward me, he told me how Ceysûr had been born with an evil heart, how he had killed the boy because it was feared that Ceysûr would lead his mother and father, both devout believers, astray from the righteous path, how he didn't commit this murder of his own will. When he said this, my heart broke asunder, and blood seeped into my soul.

—

Let's say that you're pregnant, and you have a dream three days before you're due to give birth. Let's say that in the dream, a white-bearded old man with a voice like thunder tells you that you are going to bear a boy, that when this boy grows up he will become a crueler person than any tyrant who ever lived, that he will madly believe that his lineage is the most advanced race and, that in order to establish a homeland for the Aryan people that resembles the city of Sparta, he begins by killing the physically and mentally disabled, followed by the Romani, the Jews, the Kurds, the Alevis, the Armenians, the Assyrians, and the Greeks; let's say you awaken with your heart in your throat, haunted by the divination that your still-unborn son will lay waste to the world; let's say you begin to doubt yourself, shamefully wishing that you wouldn't give birth, that you would miscarry; let's say that after birth, caressing the baby's nut-colored hair as you nurse him on your breast, that you begin to soften, that you realize he knows nothing yet apart from your breast; let's say you find yourself crying out of turn because you can't tell anyone about the dream, which sometimes returns, its terrorizing fervor tearing through the membrane of his gentleness; let's say that you then begin to go mad under the weight of this burden, you simply can't bear it, and let's say that the nights perpetually remind you of his slaughters; let's say you, a woman feeling postpartum pain in her groin, look murderously upon the baby, your baby, in its cradle in those hours when everyone is asleep; how could you possibly break out of this hellish impasse? To consider that a little death, a single snap of his tiny neck, a smothering against your breast, could save millions of people... But since your son can't kill those millions on his own, won't you also have to kill the many people who vest him with the authority to do so? What I mean is that, behind those seven veils, I saw Hızır, and I also saw the impossibility of being Hızır. There was really only one Hızır. Only one Hızır who, manifesting as someone else, lay to waste the sum of human morality... Only one Hızır who, afraid of what was going to happen, spilled the blood of a future tyrant, of the innocent Ceysûr of the present, only one Hızır who forced me to reckon with the potential that you, too, could commit murder... To look at Hızır through Hızır's eyes dazzled me, subsumed me in a white blindness. The person standing behind those seven veils was unequivocally a child murderer, the catalyst of that child's death, yet he was the only immortal wandering the earth, and he had surrendered himself to fear.

—

When he took his second step, I saw another dimension of Hızır. There was a cold, righteous expression on his face as he tucked the bloody handkerchief back into his jacket pocket, an expression undaunted by the grisly scene behind him. He now stood behind six veils. I realized then that Hızır had no freewill. You remember the young man whose picture you took in Izmir, sitting by himself outside of a coffeehouse covered in wisteria? In spite of his youth, the eyes that stared into your lens were aged. His shoulders slumped, as if he had surrendered his entire being to the world. That's exactly what Hızır looked like: that young man in the instant you took his photograph so long ago. He seemed to have no need for morality, no need for reason, for conscience, for principles. Utterly lacking a will of his own, fettered to the mandate he carried in his soul, he was bound to the will of a divine being. A will that manifested itself in this act, a will that runs the risk of terror. Hızır was nothing, nothing, nothing but the agent of this will. Such acts were testament to his exaltation and his faith in this will; he wandered the earth, an elusive stranger among us, gleaning salvation from cruelty, love from hate, kindness from calamity.

—

When he took his next step, I saw the decisive moments of others written upon his face. Resigned to his fate, like the Xanthian soldiers who burned their families to death in the agora, like Celal who murdered his children, he proceeded calmly, his arms hanging limp by his sides, a mournful expression on his face. He had surrendered himself to all the affairs of the world. In his furrowed brow, I read that freewill can only flourish in the cradle of fate.

—

After Hızır took another step, the ambivalence on his face started to disappear. He was sepia behind those four veils. His expressive gaze made me recognize that everything I saw there was nothing more than a representation, that the realm of the seen isn't all it appears to be. The corpse of Ceysûr had disappeared from the foot of the wall. In reality, no murder had taken place. All that blood, that violence, limbs thrashing in the air, pain-filled gurgles, were merely Hızır's own self-destruction. Because Ceysûr's body was the abode of insatiable delights. Ceysûr was an effigy of Hızır's immaturity, his unappeasable desires. Killing Ceysûr was how he extirpated these desires by the root. It was how he snuffed out the devil cloaked in a mask of innocence, beating its head against the wall. In a way, Hızır demonstrated how to turn away from the deceptive beauty of worldly manifestations, a beauty that corrodes the spirit. By attenuating that which attenuated him, he opened up a wound in his very being, a wound in the shape of Ceysûr, and he was dying and being reborn, slouching slowly toward me, there, in the dark.

———

When he passed through the fourth veil and reached the third, the scent of his sweat reached my nose. The scent reminded me of your own. Clearly, Hızır is also an aesthetic figure. He is the hidden face you look for in photographs, he comes to life in the language of poets, he is an obedient character responsible for articulating the endlessness of the conscious mind, a vassal who bears no trace of happiness or misfortune. He is ready to do your bidding, held in the yoke of unconditional fidelity. As if it were not enough to burden him with all the fantasies, some sacred and some profane, that originate in your dark passions, he was also how you tasted the feeling of yearning for someone lost, the feeling of bewilderment at the unknowable limit of human brutality, the feeling of wonder at a spider weaving its web, weaving order into life. You've always brought up Hızır as the key to preventing forgetfulness, always used him to shroud the ghastly memory of the massacre, or perhaps it was yourself you shrouded, in the same way your grandmother did. And you've always secretly envied Hızır the abilities you'd never possess. You've wasted your time chasing after a legendary hero who could see everything, who could be anywhere at any time. Trailing that agent of God, you've been left dumbfounded, lacking an agency of your own. Yet it was you who pulled his strings. It was your long shadow, fettered to your body, cast upon the veils between

you and him. That phantom could never be detached
from you.

Hızır appeared in his true colors when there were
two veils left between us; his skin the dull matte of
ordinary skin, the deep lines on his forehead suddenly
clear. My heart beat in the pure reality of this moment.
Hızır wasn't really looking at me. His eyes were on
mine, but his gaze saw someone else. He seemed to
be standing in the depths of a dark forest, beneath a
canopy of intertwining pine branches, his neck tense,
his focus somewhere else, off in the distance. He was
watching a small group of people, their backs to the
volcanic rocks just past the edge of the forest. Forty
people, forty grieving people, their clothes shorn,
their skin lacerated from dragging themselves across
the jagged crust of the earth. Among them was a man
with one eye bandaged, the other bloody, calling to
Hızır with words that burned in the air. Hızır was listening to the quivering lamentation of this man who
resisted the urge to condemn, and as he listened, he
stood in place, inert, his air of loneliness compounded
by the fact that he found everything that had happened in Dersim entirely ordinary. I saw, in the way
his lips twisted to the left, that he had noticed a girl
who had found solace in his dominion. A girl sitting
where I stood, so close to the flames she might catch

fire, rocking back and forth, bent in on herself like a bug that curls up in defense when you touch it. Hızır was calling Bese to him, Bese who had saved herself from the clotted waters of the Munzur, Bese who still heard the whistle of bullets in her ears. With a sibyllic smile on his lips, he watched, pleased, as the girl brushed off her ragged skirts, stood up, and approached him.

I was two veils apart from Hızır. Two steps, the distance from here to there. But they were two steps that neither Hızır nor I could not take. Neither one of us could have stepped into Bese's path. From time immemorial we have been divided by an intimacy that could never have included us.

When I left Hızır, strangely enough, I didn't feel a sense of loss. We parted ways without farewells. As I turned my back and departed, I didn't even pause to wonder whether he was watching after me. Near daybreak, I began to climb the hill from Galata to Beyoğlu. It was only then that I noticed the various insignia left in the façades of the historic buildings that had once been inhabited by Greek families. It seems you only ever walk through here with your head down, your senses closed off. It seems you've been living the life of gods and ghosts, a life without touching, without penetrating into the textures of the world. It seems your skulking shame has distracted all your senses. It seems your passions are forbidden, your dreams fraudulent. It seems you've been in a deep sleep, in a cradle of fantasy that has smothered the violence of your emotions. Perhaps one morning, if you're not too lazy, you should head up to Beyoğlu, so you might get a sense of the life you haven't been a part of, the smell of alcohol wafting through side streets, the heaps of filth in corners, the nylon bags soaring in the morning breeze, the beer cans you have to kick out of your way at every step, the cigarette butts, the carnations that the flower-sellers thrust in your face, the loose change lost by street musicians, the food containers, the crumpled newspapers, all those things that have been dropped, lost, or tossed aside, all those things that reveal to you just how late you are in coming here, all those new encounters and infatuations and embraces, all those huddled conversations, the piss-drunk buffoonery and the disagreements over misplaced words, the mistakes and the mending of mistakes and the settling of accounts, the outright fights raised by challenges and the annoying curiosity of strangers, all the traces of your absence, traces you would never have thought to photograph... I'm getting ahead of myself, I'm sorry, but this is why you've never succeeded as a photographer, never been able to move people's hearts: your inability to remove the poetic template of some spiritual reality from this damnable world.

—

Just before I arrived here at your house, I saw a man. A real man! He has a carpentry shop in Çukurcuma. I was headed down to Karaköy on my way to Beşiktaş when I heard the distant sound of a band saw and changed my direction. The sound was coming from a dingy shop down a set of stairs. It was around six in the morning. None of the other shops, which sold antiques and had ornate, wrought iron window grilles, had yet opened up for the day. I descended the stairs and came to the door. The carpenter was a formidable man with greying hair, working among the mottled plumes of light plunging into the shop from the small window in the back. Thanks to the light, I could see the vapor emanating from the man's body. There was a rough-hewn piece of timber in front of him. I watched as he passed the wood through the saw, saw how the wood shavings flew into the air, glimmering as they fell to the ground, the dust of trees raining gently down. I could tell by the smell of the dust that it was a cherry tree he had split through. The man's calloused hands had committed the cherry tree to memory, learned it by heart. He handled the timber with the tree's temperament, steadfast and reverent, offering his gratitude and esteem as he passed it through the saw. His left foot stood squarely in front of him, his right positioned so as to balance the tips of his fingers. He leaned slightly forward, licking his lips from time to time. In spite of his thirst, he didn't stop working. On the wall across from him hung a picture of a little girl wearing a school uniform. Her gentle smile could occasionally be glimpsed through the timber leaning against the wall. A smile in an old frame, hazy behind the blurred glass. Was she the carpenter's daughter, and if she was, where was she now, all grown up? I stood there for a long time as I watched the carpenter. He had dedicated his entire being to the tree. An incandescent and essential unity, free of reason or worry. His concentration was so intense he hardly even blinked. As the wood dust accrued on his head and shoulders, he slowly came to resemble the cherry tree itself. Nothing, nothing, nothing but an agent of the tree, without the augury of any god. And I, too, was nothing, nothing, nothing but an agent of my curiosity, watching a carpenter who entrusted his faith to the cherry tree.

I rushed here to you just so I could tell you about this moment. In fact, this was where I wanted to begin; I was going to tell you how deftly the carpenter stopped time. But when I found you there in bed like that, doubled over, squeezing your fists tight, I had to change the order of my story. The milky ghosts of the clear sky passed through your tulle curtains, kissed your bare arms. Your body was rolled into a ball. Folded in on yourself in a moment of timid prudence, you traced the shape of shame with your body, concealing that feeling as it pulled you into its center. You were seeking a language for yourself, a language inherited from no one and akin to no one else's, a language of figs… You were you, ready to pass through me. Like the tree that spawns its own leaves, you were the words that expressed yourself.

—

I can't explain to you how hard it is to tell this story, to unpeel it for you, word by word. For years, I have wandered the tunnels inside you, kept in thrall by your shame. This vexing story has taken so long, it has been like waiting for fruit to ripen. Even the work of carving gems from rock cannot compare with the journey that shame takes to reach language. Because the tongue gets tied. Because children like you, born into the silence that remains after catastrophe, are born unable to cry out. Even if misery comes undone in language, even if wistfulness gives you pleasure, even if grief makes you feel that you matter, still, shame will always settle like a stone in your gut. The sheer horror in the scene of a massacre, in the killing of one person by another, can never be contained in a photograph.

Your body's dignity is delicate, diaphanous like vellum. It gets torn apart, end to end, by a contemptuous shove, by the piercing of a bayonet, the jolt of a pistol, the barrel of a machine gun. What's left over is your sensitive spirit, scabbing over with shame. So forgive me, I can't speak like everyone else. I can't form long, winding sentences that can explain away the historic trajectory of this emotion I carry. All I can do is beseech with sighs, lament with wails, freeze up in bewilderment. I can speak in metaphorical language about the hollow left when human dignity is torn from its roots. Be grateful that Bese left you not with the bruises of her affliction, but with the shame of being human, a shame that grows in the aftermath of ruin. Your shame is a veneration of what it means to be alive. It is the singular foundation of the person you have become. I don't know if you realize it, but you began healing the moment you were born.

—

So let me go now, back to my home, back to the inchoate world of words. It's cold out. Let me come face to face with you, climb through your mouth and back inside you. Let me find myself a place upon your face, somewhere I can stretch out, where I can reach for where you ache. If you're going to arrange sentences one after the other, write them on your own flesh, just don't touch mine. This time, you speak, I'll listen. Let's commiserate with one another, with no witnesses. Take responsibility for the sin of every punctuation mark, choose a different path than Bese's for yourself. Since you can never take Bese's final two steps, dwell instead on who she was before Hızır. Find affinity with your grandmother's spirit, free of faith and anguish. Look in your breast for the innocence of a moth drawn to the flame, of a fish bleeding for the silkworm on the fishing hook. Consider the partridge ensnared on birdlime, compare its mistake with your shame. Let me watch how they go, with their naïve illusions, how this allegory of your existence passionately burns, and burns, and in the end, burns out.

And don't forget, even Jesus, that runic man of

miracles, that son of God who brought the dead to life with his touch, even he looked far off into the distance and saw a ripe fig tree, with its water-green leaves, swaying in the breeze on the side of the road. His apostles were at his side. When he saw the tree, I suppose his mouth must have watered. He must have craved a fig, suddenly aware of the exhaustion he felt after delivering sermons under the hot sun for days on end. He hurried toward the tree to eat a couple of its fruits. But when he reached it, he saw not a single fig on its branches. Jesus had apparently crossed paths with a male fig tree. But Jesus, perhaps because he was Jesus, disregarding the fact that his appetite had drawn him to the tree, disregarding the deceptive and dizzying allure of his appetite, disregarding even that life desires survival before it desires the heart's mercy, raised the staff in his hand and cursed the tree. The fig tree withered instantly at Jesus' word. The tree, then, listened to the word, so docile it didn't hold Jesus' innocent mistake against him; the tree, which did not deserve the prophet's fury, which had not even tried to be a prophet itself, knew to die there where it stood, with inimitable simplicity.

It's clear that in your sleep, you dreamed of being a prophet. For so long, you have had delusions of moral grandeur. Babbling to a tree that listens to human speech, you've mired yourself in a swamp of loneliness. And to use the branches of your miraculous fig to try and pull yourself out is unforgivable. Knowing full well the repugnance of every name you levied at it, you fell short as soon as you began to hope that the fig could ever be human.

Because the fig
suffices unto itself. Calmly, it becomes itself.
Whereas human spirit
Is scattered far and wide.
Let's the two of us, you and me,
Gather it up as we march toward death.

—

AFTERWORD:
A LANGUAGE OF FIGS

Like everyone, I too am made of language. I remember how I came into being like it was yesterday: as a single sentence, head to toe. One day, my mother told me she felt the seed take root the instant I flashed like a spark in her womb, when my father whispered into her ear, "A girl." I felt an unbridled sense of gratitude as I listened to this story, felt the joy of being beckoned lovingly into this world. From that day forth, I gained a newfound respect for all the creatures I encountered in the world, each bestowed with its own unique significance. That sentence of hers had planted itself in my spirit to such a degree that I was carried away imagining my mother during her pregnancy, imagining her craving moonlight and my father gathering moonlight for her accordingly. To imagine was, if nothing else, to hold my place in the world.

And yet, there was another sentence: "They

slaughtered us," my grandmother once said. We just sat there afterward, our sighs resounding. She didn't say anything else, didn't offer any details or explanations. This time, a historic pain, incompletely mourned, began etching itself into my bones.

What's interesting is that up until that moment, I had no social identity, no nation, no homeland, but I did have a world. Within the meandering rift between the world and my parents, I had been living in a time-span unsullied by others. Each and every word was to me a fleeting, limpid, lyrical sound. But after I heard "they slaughtered us," all the words I knew began to harden. The fearless fantasies my imagination nourished were suddenly sullied by the injured expressions of an outsider. It was as though I was a fruit with two seeds and a bitter rind. From one seed sprouted words to consecrate what it meant to be alive; from the other, execrable sorrow. I was made of their language: shaped by my mother's tone of voice, silenced by my grandmother's taciturn manner, I was imprisoned in a rhetorical bind, as everyone is, between life and despair.

The first hard word I ever encountered was "impossibility:" the impossibility of sharing the stories told at home with others. I would listen to my grandmother tell various parables rooted in her Alevi faith, only to be forcefully admonished afterward that I ought not to tell others what I'd heard. This was a kind of training in the art of silence. I will not speak at length about how corrosive it has felt to hide that my family are the descendants of the Alevi exiles of Dersim, in particular because my father was an officer and we lived covertly as a religious minority in a military environment, in a hierarchical community that is the state's singular stronghold for the pure Turkish-Sunni identity. Turkey's one-nation ideology insists upon the uniform homogeneity of all citizens as the foundation of its Republican revolution; this ideology has so flagrantly failed to stand the test of time that we ought to set aside complaining about it and inaugurate a new time altogether. Because every complaint and denunciation, every language of Otherhood established in opposition to this homogeneity, has the potential to evolve with every passing day into a discourse that promotes further militarism. If nothing else, I refuse any nationalist the right to speak on my behalf. The best way to unshackle the discourses of freedom and justice from the snare of one culture, one minority, one religion, or one people, is to let them speak in opposition, simultaneously with everyone and as everyone, without attempting to assume power. This plural language, in my opinion, is so emancipatory that it does not merely compel domestic silence out into the open; it also attaches the language in which that silence belongs to all languages, to all humanity.

I know from my grandmother how pain gives way to silence. And yet, though she was a master of silence, she spoke all the time. That woman constantly talked about her impoverished childhood, about the older sister she lost at a young age, about the many djinns, spirits, and beings from the other world whom she saw in her dreams. She would relay her profound wisdom to us, telling us how to pick tobacco leaves, about the healing power of linden, the misery of kneading bread, the way that every drop of water turns to steam and returns to the earth. And she would pair everything in the world up with something else. Just as she paired a star in the sky with a rock on the ground, or mountain with sea, or lake with desert, she paired me with the fig tree in her garden, insisting that the fig tree was my sister. Despite her ceaseless oratory, though, she never once spoke about all the killing she witnessed in Dersim in 1937 and 1938. She had survived one of the most gruesome massacres in the history of the Republic of Turkey, had been torn from her family and exiled from her home, and yet she never once looked back at Dersim, never made mention of it. Even as my grandmother shared all her wisdom about the world, she remained silent about Dersim. Why? What would a person who spoke so much choose to keep silent? Perhaps what kept my grandmother silent was her fear; perhaps it was her solemnity that would not condescend to the language of victimhood; or perhaps, most probably, it was her shame. It was the deep guilt of having survived that hell, a hell that lasted only a few months but in which thousands of people were killed and exiled. It was the shame of being human. It was the insurmountable horror she felt in the face of what mankind does to one another. In another sense, it was her willful forgetting, a way to resist making meaning out of cruelty. Beyond all of this, however, what left her speechless was the sheer futility of speaking in the name of the dead—the people bayonetted, raked by machine guns, abased, poisoned with gas, pushed off cliffs, burned to death in haylofts, the lost community for whom saying "They slaughtered us" could simply never suffice. The fact is, the true witnesses of Dersim were the dead, and they will never be able to speak again. What haunts me most, though what my grandmother left me with, is not simply the fact that I was born, but that I descended from her loins, alive. I have a home where I was never born, languages which I never learned, relatives whom I mourn without having ever known them. Even if I wrote for a lifetime, I don't think I could ever fill that deep void.

In truth, I never really knew my grandmother. I had neither religion like hers to chasten the anguish she left me, nor faith like hers to pair up all the things in the world. What eventually opened up the depths of her spirit to me was Hızır, her god. Without Hızır, the principal deity to the Alevis of Dersim, I would never have been able to fully understand my grandmother's refuge of silence, her determined lack of anger, which she buoyed with constant prayer and benediction. Hızır was, for her, a symbol of poetic justice; he was an immortal being who could emerge in any place at any time, who appeared and disappeared at a moment's notice, who shifted from one guise to another, who knew the cause of all things past and future. My grandmother regarded every downtrodden person she encountered as Hızır, feeding them, comforting them, and bidding them farewell on their return to the Barzakh, that purgatory between life and death. She treated every beggar like a wounded god, thus pairing up her god with the poor and the hungry; she looked upon strangers as though they were manifestations of the divine. She had nobody else left except her faithful companion, "O Hızır," as she tended to address him.

In the Al-Kahf surah of the Quran, which narrates the journey the prophet Moses takes with Hızır, Moses is characterized almost as a pupil. Before they embark on their journey, Hızır advises Moses to be patient and not to ask questions in all the situations they will encounter. For Moses, this ends up being a rather difficult journey, because Hızır does a number of unexpected things, damaging the boat of a poor man who aided them, and killing a young boy. In so doing, Hızır serves as a figure who not only tries Moses' patience, but demolishes his concept of earthly justice as well. According to Islamic theology, Hızır is neither saint nor prophet, neither angel nor dervish, and yet he is all of these at once. Beginning life as the Sumerian god Tammuz, and continuing as a soldier who drank the water of life while on Alexander's campaign in India, even manifesting in the paintings of Marc Chagall, Hızır has wandered the four corners of the earth under an endless array of guises and names, appearing, finally, before my grandmother, as a poor and wounded man.

This novel stands as a question mark that opens the threshold onto this corrupted world, precisely as it was seen by Hızır and my grandmother. If what we call the novel is an art, then at the same time it is a chamber with two doors that declares a secret undisclosable, that maps safe country for all the exiles of the world, wandering in search of their place. I have reserved a place here for my grandmother, yet I haven't managed to fit it onto a single page, the shame of being human that she left to me. The more I explored the details of the Dersim Massacre, the heartrending photographs and historical documents that came to light, the more I have come to refuse the notion of inuring the reader to this violence, by making a novel about how this massacre began and how it ended, by portraying these people, already so horribly dehumanized, as if this were their only fate, their only essence, frozen in place and time.

I know from the start that for many this approach might go too far. Given that the first reaction of a society indoctrinated by the lies of official history is to deny and even to blame the victims without mercy, writing a novel about Dersim that spoke to this majority would have been both more sensible and more utilitarian. But when a writer falls in line with the dominant ways of thinking in her country, the first thing she loses is the creative impulse that beckons her to speak authentically, in her own voice. To me, it seems necessary to add to the corpus of world literature, which enumerates the irreparable wounds of genocide and massacre, the solemn consolations an exile offered herself, whether or not they are ever accorded any value.

Adorno once wrote that there can be no poetry after Auschwitz. For some reason, everyone remembers this sentence. Yet fewer ever remember the figure of Paul Celan, the incomparable German poet who survived in a concentration camp, or his "Death Fugue," which proclaims the insurmountable power of poetry for and by a people facing indiscriminate erasure. Following Celan's response to Adorno, the philosopher gradually changed his opinion that poetry could never be written again, submitting that the poems of Celan express the most unimaginable horror with profound quietude. In my opinion, the fate of Celan and others like him serves to chronicle the same suffering experienced in Dersim. If the many agonies of the people of Dersim still don't seem legible to some readers, despite the extensive corpus decrying the suffering inflicted on humanity—and thus on all creatures of the earth and sky—I cannot do anything else except encourage them to imagine themselves as Jews, Armenians, Aboriginal peoples, Native Americans, Bosnians, Khojaly Azerbaijanis, Tutsis, or Darfuris.

Finally, I would like to say, I intended to write

Every Fire You Tend not just in Turkish, but in the language of all who lament for the dead. And I intended to write it with the language of figs, which I grasped by looking at my sister, at the fig tree whose fruit has, over the course of the history of civilization, seduced and destroyed, poisoned and healed, struck panic in those captivated by its pleasure, and been served like jewels at the tables of kings, pharaohs, and sultans— in order that I might set aside its vitalizing force, its enviable adventure, in writing. What I mean to say is that, over the course of this novel, I am not only my grandmother who survived the massacre: I am also her granddaughter, I am Hızır, and I am a fig, with its countless tiny seeds. Each of us has written the others into being.

TRANSLATOR'S NOTE

There is no such place as Dersim—at least, this is what the official story would have you believe. You will not find it in any government document, in any tourist guide, on any map, in any textbook; it is as if Dersim does not exist, as if it has never existed. And yet, the "perennial Dersim question" has weighed on Turkey's official history ever since the establishment of the Republic in 1923.[1]

The cadre of nationalists who founded the nascent nation-state, led by Mustafa Kemal Atatürk, enacted aggressive policies of linguistic, ethnic, cultural, and religious homogenization in the pursuit of secular, liberal modernity. Dersim, however, served as an inexorable thorn in their side, practically impossible to assimilate not merely due to its remoteness high in the Taurus Mountains nor simply its significant Zaza-

---

1 Zeynep Türkyılmaz, "Maternal Colonialism and Turkish Woman's Burden in Dersim: Educating the 'Mountain Flowers' of Dersim," *Journal of Women's History* 28, no. 3 (2016): 164.

speaking Kurdish and Alevi minorities, but also by virtue of its long-standing tradition of resisting state instrumentalization, as when Dersim's tribal groups offered refuge and safe passage to Armenians fleeing the Armenian genocide. In December 1935, two years before the military campaign against Dersim began in earnest, the Turkish Parliament changed the official name of the region from Dersim (Persian for "silver door") to Tunceli (Turkish for "bronze city"). They also replaced the Armenian, Kurdish, and Zaza names of the region's towns and cities with Turkish ones, all in an effort to constrain and contain the insurgency of these languages and populations that refused to be assimilated. The carpet-bombing campaigns of 1937 and 1938 marked the culmination of this campaign to wipe Dersim and its unruly populations off the map.

It is no coincidence that the very same ideologues who planned and executed the Dersim massacre had, less than a decade earlier, embarked on an ambitious campaign to reform the Turkish language, to make it simultaneously modern and vernacular by abandoning the Arabic script in favor of the Latin, and by excising Persian and Arabic loanwords in favor of Turkish neologisms and French borrowings. The language's "extreme self-surgery"[2] was aided and abetted

---

2   Nergis Ertürk, *Grammatology and Literary Modernity in Turkey* (London: Oxford University Press, 2012), 87.

by popular public campaigns, such as the "Citizen, Speak Turkish!" (*Vatandaş Türkçe Konuş!*) campaign of the late 1920s and 1930s, to patrol and subdue the use of Kurdish, Greek, Armenian, Ladino, Arabic, and other languages. Turkish nationalist literature of the time symbolically marked the use of "non-national non-Turkish" languages as dangerous and deadly.[3] To speak them, or to be seduced by their use, was understood to endanger the sanctity and ongoing life of the Turkish nation. This rhetorical move consolidated the central value of pure Turkish to the nationalist project; at the same time, it consigned these other languages, and their speakers, to obsolescence and obliteration.

I begin with this history because I think it offers some insight into the stakes of Kaygusuz's writerly choices, both in terms of style and structure. As such, it serves as a lens through which to explore some of the unique challenges and obstacles that I've faced while translating this novel, which is so self-consciously about the failures and excesses of language and its capacity, or incapacity, to represent reality. How to translate a novel about the violent colonization of Dersim in the past, a novel written in the colonizers' language, from a future in which colonization seems to have all but prevailed, and in

---

3   Nergis Ertürk, *Grammatology and Literary Modernity in Turkey* (London: Oxford University Press, 2012), 93.

which the Zaza language spoken in Dersim is considered an endangered language? How to translate the histories of violence in a world where language has "dried up"? How to capture this novel's repertoire of sensuous intensities, written in "a language inherited from no one and akin to no one else's"?

Every Fire You Tend is peppered with Ottoman-era literary flourishes that seem, to the Turkish reader, anachronistic. Kaygusuz told me that she composed the text with a Turkish-Ottoman dictionary by her side. The particular stylistic effect of this willful obfuscation is not simply to imbue the prose with an antiquated tone, as if it were being narrated by a grandparent or an elderly relative; it is also to foreground the linguistic and cultural intimacy that Turkish still shares with Arabic, Persian, and Kurdish, and in so doing, to show how the Turkish language continues to be haunted by all the multivalent elements that language reformers and subsequent nationalists tried to exterminate. Kaygusuz's anachronisms erupt through the lush prose of the novel, puncturing the ideological fabric that bounds the Turkish linguistic nation in space and time.

In one such passage, the protagonist visits the ruins of the ancient city of Xanthos, drawn to its history of mass suicide in the face of a potential subjection. She reflects on the fact that, over the centuries, the different populations that inhabited the city each brought upon themselves the same fate as their predecessors.

İhtişamlı bir misillemenin yuvası olarak tarihe geçen Ksanthos'ta tek bir Likyalı kalmamış olması, özkıyım olarak hatırlanabilir elbette. Ama niyeyse aşırı bir gurur misali olarak anılıyor. Sanki iki ayrı kan damlası var damardan fışkıracak. Biri Likyalının iyi şiddetini, öbürü Harpagos'un kötü şiddetini temsil ediyor. Sonradan şehre yerleşen başka halklar, Ksanthosluların yok oluş tarihlerinden öylesine etkilenirler ki bu onurlu şiddet masalı sürekli tavaf edilen ruhsal bir mabet haline gelir.

Xanthos passed into the annals of history as the home of this kind of solemn reprisal, and the fact that not a single Lycian survived means that it is remembered for this act of total self-destruction. Yet for some reason, this story is always characterized as an illustration of the repercussions of excessive pride. As if there were two kinds of blood that could be spilled, one representing the righteous violence of the Lycians; the other, Harpagos's wicked violence. Other peoples who later settled in the city were so affected by the history of the Xanthians' obliteration that this fearsome and violent tale became sacred, worthy of their unceasing devotion.

The words indicated in this passage can be translated as follows:

misilleme: reprisal, reiteration, retort, derived from *misil*, meaning counterpart, analogue, iteration

misal: exemplar, epitome, illustration

temsil: representation, rendition

masal: tale, story, fable, legend

All of these words are loanwords from Arabic in that they share a common root, *m–s–l* (vernacularized from the standard Arabic *m–th–l*), meaning "to resemble, to be or look like someone, to bear a likeness to, to imitate or copy." The Arabic language, like other Semitic languages, is built around a system of lexical roots out of which words are formed. Each root can be transposed into set patterns, including verbal conjugations, verbal nouns, and participles, to produce variant meanings. In practice, this means that words have connotative resonance by virtue of their shared root, refracting affectively off one another, even where their denotative definitions might significantly diverge—especially in translation. The motif of resemblance and imitation echoes gently across the sentences in this passage, as the style of the novel comes to mirror its content: stories of past violence reverberate outward across time, recurring over and over, weighing unbearably on the present, as if we have no choice but to reenact those stories, as if our futures inevitably echo our darkest pasts. The novel is replete with similar instances in which non-Turkish words punctuate the flow of the Turkish prose, and while their presence breathes a symphonic quality into the novel, they have nonetheless been the hardest to capture in English translation. Like Sema, I embarked on my translation with a retinue of reference works: several Turkish-English dictionaries, an Ottoman-Turkish dictionary, an Arabic-English dictionary, and an English thesaurus, in order to try to achieve something of her antiquated and idiosyncratic tone.

With the previous passage, for example, I tried to achieve something of the original not through my translation of the words *misilleme*, *misal*, *temsil*, and *masal*, but by rendering other words as "reprisal, remember, repercussion, represent," to reiterate a similarly recursive and uncannily resonant effect. But what, after all, is the original? If I had wanted to produce a "faithful translation," I would have had to attend to the many linguistic intimacies that are legible to the Turkish reader in the original. I would have to communicate centuries' worth of Ottoman literary traditions, vernaculars that freely imbricated Turkish, Arabic, Persian, and Kurdish tropes and words, playing with the limits and possibilities of each grammar and syntax. I would have had to convey the vernacularized multilingualism that has been a hallmark of Anatolian society since time immemorial. In short, I would have had to express an entire history of cross-cultural communication and exchange that the nationalists tried to meticulously and violently homogenize and manage, a history that surges up as a "seething presence"[4] in this novel. Would such a translation have been more or less palatable to the reader? Would I have done this novel a service or a disservice had I strived for this kind of faithfulness? If fiction is "an act of speaking otherwise,"[5] is it possible to translate the "otherwise" of one language into another?

What I find most striking about the specter of Arabic in the excerpt here is that these words, and the root they come from, have to do with the concepts of representation, resemblance, repetition. Questions of representation, resemblance, and repetition are at the very heart of this novel, and they open up another set of obstacles I faced in the translation process. I examine these obstacles now by tracing, again, the echoes of the *m–s–l* root across the text, but it is certainly not the only such Arabic root bridging the form and content of this work. Tracing other Arabic roots—particularly *ş–h–d*, to witness, *z–l–m*, to treat unjustly, and *r–h–m*, to be merciful—along with the additional non-Turkish linguistic elements scattered in this novel, is a task I leave to a more skilled linguist.

---

4   Avery Gordon, *Ghostly Matters: Haunting and the Sociological Imagination* (Minneapolis: University of Minnesota Press, 2008), 195.

5   Nergis Ertürk, *Grammatology and Literary Modernity in Turkey* (London: Oxford University Press, 2012), 81.

—

The novel is woven together by a threadwork of tales, or *masal*, as in the previous passage. The reader encounters the narrator, "yoked by the tales" she herself ties together in her address to the main character, and we hear the tale of Eliha and the tale of Sultan Suleiman in the boat. We meet Bese, who lives in a "fabled abode" (*masalsı yuva*) in Samsun, and who tells the tale of Zulqarnayn and the stones that turn to gold. We're made aware of the "morality tale" (*ibretlik bir masal*) of the cuckoo bird "stuck in [the] throats" of the exiles of Dersim. And Hızır, too, is a figure "sprung from the sanguine legends [*masallar*] of the spring festivals."

Hızır weaves "a web" of such tales "across time," manifesting the inexorable force of the past in the stultified time of the present, and as such he serves as a linchpin that ties together the novel's questions of representation, resemblance, and repetition, by straddling the many different forms taken by the *m–s–l* root. Near the end of the novel, Hızır looks at the narrator with a gaze that makes her "recognize that everything I saw there was nothing more than a representation [*temsil*], that the realm of the seen isn't all it appears to be." He serves as a representative (*temsilci*) of God on earth—"nothing, nothing, nothing, but the agent of this will"—yet when he adopts a human guise, he wears "one of many faces in order to approach people as a friend." And he makes his repeated appearances across history "in times of extreme difficulty and debilitating indigence, in places where death made its rounds."

These concepts of representation, resemblance, and repetition do not simply animate the formal and stylistic features of this novel; they also illuminate the theology of Hızır and the Islamic mysticism central to the beliefs of the Dersim Alevis, who follow a theology called *Raa Haq* (Zaza for "true path"). To be sure, much of this theological material would be relatively unfamiliar to the typical Turkish reader, due in part to the marginalized status of Alevis in Turkey, but I want to review it here nonetheless because it sheds further light on the ways in which the form and the content of this novel are intertwined.

Medieval Muslim exegetes like Shahāb al-Dīn Suhrawardī and Ibn al-'Arabī have theorized the existence of the *'ālam al-mithāl*, a realm which lies (as the *barzakh*, that is, the isthmus or interval) in between the (at least) two other spheres of "existence," the "realm of spirits" (*'ālam al-ruḥ*) and the "realm of matter" (*'ālam al-khalq*). In their interpretations of the Qur'an they also insist that the realm of matter is broken into "seven tiers of heaven and seven tiers of

earth," each abiding by its own temporal and physi-
cal laws and populated by different and unimaginable
creatures and peoples.

'*Ālam al-mithāl*, rendered in Turkish as *misal âlemi*,
has been translated into English under such esoteric
names as the "realm of suspended forms," the "realm
of image exemplars," the "realm of pure figures,"
"the world of similitudes," "Nowhereland," and the
"imaginal realm," the latter being how I have translated it here, in order to capture the convergence of its
simultaneously imaginary and imagistic nature. The
imaginal realm is both more immaterial than the realm
of bodies and less immaterial than the realm of souls;
it is the realm in which spiritual realities are made
manifest, projected as reflections in a mirror, prefig-
uring all that is destined to happen in the worldly
realm of humans, from the miraculous and the escha-
tological to the mundane. It is the "plane of ghosts, of
the forms in mirrors, dreams, and worlds of wonder
beyond our own."[6] Our world is simply a translation,
an unveiling, of these images and imaginings.

Hızır "dwells in the imaginal realm [*misal âlemi*]
between worldly life and the afterlife," and it is where
he calls the pious, the pure, and the wayward, that
they might experience divine illumination. But the

---

6   John Walbridge, *The Leaven of the Ancients: Suhrawardī and the
    Heritage of the Greeks* (Albany: SUNY Press, 2000), 26.

imaginal realm is also open to spiritual aspirants, those who are able to close out the phenomenal world of the senses and tap into their imaginal faculty. On the very first page of this novel, the narrator tries to fend off "all those intimations of the world," her spirit having "departed to another plane altogether." She finds herself in the imaginal realm every time she awakens, when she is caught in a state between sleep and wakefulness.[7] The entire function of the narrator's fabulous digressions and elliptical tales—if there is indeed a function—might arguably be for the protagonist to "find solace in the imaginal realm [stories] create."

If the imaginal realm is both a realm for storytelling and a realm that actively prefigures the world and ushers it into being, then *Every Fire You Tend* testifies to the force that stories about the crushing weight of the past can have in shaping the face of the present, along with the potential they hold to usher in differ-

---

7   Ibn al-'Arabī writes that "The only reason God placed sleep in the animate world was so that everyone might witness the Presence of Imagination and know that there is another world similar to the sensory world," as quoted in William Chittick's book, *The Sufi Path of Knowledge: Ibn al-'Arabī's Metaphysics of Imagination* (Albany: SUNY Press, 1989), p. 119. My descriptions of Muslim mysticism have depended largely on Chittick's work, along with Amira El-Zein's book *Islam, Arabs, and the Intelligent World of the Jinn* and Salman H. Bashier's book *Ibn al-'Arabī's Barzakh: The Concept of the Limit and the Relationship between God and the World*. Readers who are interested in learning more about the material described here should seek these out for further reading.

ent and better futures. Only the past can free us from the past.

Yet this novel is not merely a testament to the life of the author's grandmother or to those lost in Dersim; it is not merely a story about the ongoing ruination of histories that are alive in the main character's body, of the language she was left with, of the shame ever settling "like a stone" in her gut. It is also the scene of language's insurgency, rendering the ways in which language is "a historical agent that is somehow free of human control or, better yet, that exceeds human control."[8] Turkey is a land of broken mirrors, Kaygusuz proclaimed in an interview soon after this novel was first released. *Every Fire You Tend* is a reflection of this breakage, but it is also a testament to the incipient collective struggles to reckon with the events of the past, with these histories of violence that are not yet over.[9] These histories are reflected in our languages, in the forms of the stories we write, and in the worlds we inhabit, worlds we have made and that we can unmake. What a joy it has been for me to translate this book, to toil in this unmaking.

8   Vicente L. Rafael, *Motherless Tongues: The Insurgency of Language Amid Wars of Translation* (Durham: Duke University Press, 2016), 190.

9   In May 2019, the municipal government of the Tunceli region voted to change the region's name back to Dersim. The governor of the region vetoed the idea, and administratively, Dersim remains Tunceli.

This edition published in the United Kingdom by Tilted Axis Press
in 2019. This translation was funded by Arts Council England.

This book has been selected to receive financial assistance from English
PEN's "PEN Translates" programme, supported by Arts Council
England. English PEN exists to promote literature and our understanding of it, to uphold writers' freedoms around the world, to campaign
against the persecution and imprisonment of writers for stating their
views, and to promote the friendly co-operation or writers and the free
exchange of ideas. www.englishpen.org

tiltedaxispress.com

First published 2009 in Istanbul by Doğan Kitap as *Yüzünde Bir Yer*.

ISBN (paperback)   9781911284291
ISBN (ebook)   9781911284284

A catalogue record for this book is available from the British Library.

Edited by Saba Ahmed
Cover design by Soraya Gilanni Viljoen
Typesetting and ebook production by Simon Collinson
Printed and bound by Nørhaven, Denmark.

ABOUT TILTED AXIS PRESS

Founded in 2015 and based in London, Toronto, and Seoul, Tilted Axis is a not-for-profit press on a mission to shake up contemporary international literature.

Tilted Axis publishes the books that might not otherwise make it into English, for the very reasons that make them exciting to us – artistic originality, radical vision, the sense that here is something new.

Tilting the axis of world literature from the centre to the margins allows us to challenge that very division. These margins are spaces of compelling innovation, where multiple traditions spark new forms and translation plays a crucial role.

As part of carving out a new direction in the publishing industry, Tilted Axis is also dedicated to improving access. We're proud to pay our translators the proper rate, and to operate without unpaid interns.

We hope you find this fantastic book as thrilling and beguiling as we do, and if you do, we'd love to know.

tiltedaxispress.com

@TiltedAxisPress